Christian Maturity

Christian Maturity

Bishop Jerry L. Maynard

True Vine Publishing Co.

Christian Maturity
Dr. Jerry L. Maynard, Sr.
Copyright © 2010 by
Dr. Jerry L. Maynard, Sr.
ISBN: 978-0-9826694-2-6

Published by
True Vine Publishing Co.
P.O. Box 22448
Nashville, TN. 37202
www.TrueVinePublishing.org

Scripture quotations, unless noted otherwise, are taken from the Holy Bible: King James Version.

Cover Design: HowYoung Creations
www.howyoungcreations.org

Printed in the United States of America—First Printing
For more information on the author or to order more books
contact www.CathedralPraise.org;
www.TrueVinePublishing.org

Contents

The Benefit of Christian Maturity

MORE ABOUT BISHOP JERRY L. MAYNARD

Notes

Christian

Maturity?

CHAPTER 1

Growth

When we talk about maturity, what comes to mind? Immediately we think of a small child growing from infancy to adulthood. Some of you may think of your sons whose diapers you changed and mouths you wiped clean as you spoon-fed them; and now they have grown to be successful, productive citizens with children of their own. Or you may think of the daughter—daddy's little girl— who use to hold on to your arm for safety and now would rather you drop her off at the corner than to allow her friends to see you drop her off at school.

One of the official definitions for maturity is *"the period in life after your physical growth has stopped and you are fully developed."* So here we discover maturity is the end result of a process of growth. This process for Christian maturity is one that has become highly disregarded. In the smoke and fog of charismatic preaching, emotionalism, the press for financial abundance and an ever-growing lust for position within the Church, the body of Christ has lost sight of what's important—

the fundamentals. In this chapter, and the chapters to follow, I want to go back to the basics, reintroducing God's simple plan for maturing His body. The first aspect we must reconsider is this concept of GROWTH.

Believe it or not, God has already ordained a proper order for the growth of His people, but who is responsible for that growth? Who is responsible for your growth? Does God leave it up to us—we mere mortals who vacillate between righteousness and unrighteousness? We, who God Himself declared in Genesis 6:3 *"My spirit shall not always strive with man, for that he also is flesh;"* Is this a being fit to be trusted with the job of developing the Body of Christ?

Ultimately, God is responsible for the growth of the Body. He is responsible for the natural and spiritual growth. When I say "natural" growth, I am referring to the numerical growth of the saints. As we see in Acts 2:47 *"And the Lord added to the church daily such as should be saved."* It is critical that the Church grow numerically, in fact it is the very mission of the Church. God did not save us just to provide spiritual fire insurance. Quite the opposite, God saved us so that we may bring others into the Body. And though it is our responsibility to go out and "compel" men to come to Jesus; to "teach all nations, baptizing them in the name of the Father, and of the Son, and of the Holy Ghost" (Mat. 28:19), Jesus lets us know that it is ultimately only through the Holy Ghost that men can be added to the Body: "no man can say that Jesus is the Lord, but by the Holy Ghost" (1 Cor. 12:3).

So the question begs to be answered; How does God implement the maturation—growth, development, or perfection—of the Church? Does He come down Himself and teach? Does He walk among us, stop at your houses, knock on our doors; ring our doors bell and say, "I am here to teach you so that you may grow"? No. He does not do that. Instead, we find God's plan of action for the natural and spiritual growth of the Church in Ephesians 4:11-13, which reads,

> "He (God) gave some, apostles; and some, prophets; and some evangelists; and some, pastors and teachers for the perfecting of the saints, for the work of the ministry, for the edifying of the body of Christ: Till we all come in the unity of the faith, and of the knowledge of the Son of God, unto a perfect man, unto the measure of the stature of the fullness of Christ."

God has delegated responsibility and He has given "Word ministers" for Christian maturity. Many people are so busy looking in the sky for blessings and answers to come down, but God has already given us the blessings and answers, embodied in our brothers and sisters in Christ. Let's discuss who these stewards of Christian maturity really are.

The apostle is a Word minister. Apostles establish churches. There are those who contend that there is no more need for the apostle because the Church of Jesus Christ has already been established. This could not be further from the truth. Where there is darkness within the soul of a people there is a need for the Church to be established. Although we live in the most technologically advanced era of human history; and the Word of God is preached in every corner of the world via television; there is still an astounding number of people who have never heard the Gospel and may never be reached were it not for the God-ordained work of apostles.

The apostle, however, is not stationary. He does not stay in one place. After establishing a church he moves on, and from that point the pastor takes the second leg of the maturation process. There are many people who call themselves apostles, but have never established a Church. These are not apostles. I have been used by God in the work of an apostle to establish about fifteen churches, but I know my calling is to pastor.

The pastor has to function in many categories, but mostly the Bible tells Pastors to feed the sheep. In fact, the word "Pastor" in Greek translates to "one who tends to the flock." The pastor is the protector of the Body. Although the apostle may point out the grazing grounds, and the prophets and evangelists may bring good tidings and words of encouragement and/or rebuke, it is the pastor who sees to the ultimate well being of the flock—the saints. There are some evangelists who come in and batter saints with strong words of rebuke; and because they don't know the people they are rebuking, they can sometimes leave the people disheartened without another thought of the impact they had on them. The pastor caresses you; loves you; and gives you instruction. The pastor knows the sheep.

Every once in a while the pastor has to take out that little ruler and tap your hands. An evangelist cannot do it; it's not his or her job; and not the prophet's job. That's the pastor's job to correct, to guide, to lead and do the other things necessary to help perfect you. If a child grows up in a home with parents who never give correction or constructive criticism, that child will not be perfected. Therefore, the pastor is the guardian of Christian maturity. Of course, each Christian is commanded to walk out their own salvation, but, as the parents are responsible for the home, the pastor is responsible for the Church.

However, the pastor cannot do the job on his own, therefore there are teachers, prophets, and evangelists. Teachers within the body of Christ are invaluable. Though the pastor looks over the church and leads the church, the teachers play a major role in the maturation process. Most pastors provide the weekly sermons on Sunday mornings and nights, and Wednesdays. However, that sermon must target the general assembly. The teachers within the church have the privileged benefit of targeting one focused area of study on a regular basis, which is an indispensable tool of Christian maturity.

The Church also has need of prophetic utterance. What is prophecy? The truth of God declared—whether it be that which is to come or that which is. We need that office working in the Church. Lastly, the evangelist comes to stir us up. You need stirring sometimes. The Evangelist will always confirm the message that the pastor has been providing. It always amuses me how the evangelist can preach the same sermon the pastor has been preaching for years, but it will come across as brand new. Of course, this is the nature of humanity. We tend to overlook that of which we have an abundance. Evangelists come and go, so the word they bring always seems new.

Why does God choose these ministries — the apostles, the prophets, evangelists, pastors and teachers? Why does God designate them to carry out the responsibility for perfection, for the work of the ministry, for edifying the body of Christ? He chooses them because of the fact that through divine order and spiritual authority, He equips them; He puts within their spirit a deposit of His truth that does not go out to the local congregation. You will never receive from God what God has placed in these chosen vessels. This in no way diminishes your individual anointing and portion of faith which God has given all believers. Even more, this does not suggest the man or woman that God chooses to anoint is holier than you.

I know that God speaks to you. However, He does not equip you as He equips those called to a higher position of service. More interestingly, that anointing is not contingent upon the good works of the vessel. You may be more polite, or less prone to sin than the vessel God has chosen, but God's anointing can only manifest in the vessel God has chosen. A fine example of this is found in a comparison of King David and

Uriah; Bathsheba's husband. In comparison, we find that Uriah displayed far more honor, integrity, and fidelity than King David. Yet, Uriah was not anointed king of Israel. Uriah was not given the distinguished eternal compliment as being named "a man after (God's) own heart." God's anointing is the reason we are who we are. Titles mean absolutely nothing. God does not honor the title. God only honors His anointing.

Mature to Distinguish the Truth

God gave "some" apostles, prophets, evangelists, pastors and teachers for the perfection of the saints. He gave them for the purpose of helping you not to be,

> "tossed to and fro, and carried about with every wind of doctrine, by the sleight of men and cunning craftiness, whereby they lie in wait to deceive. "
>
> —Ephesians 4:14

In order to avoid being tossed to and fro by every wind of doctrine, you have to be mature in the Word of God. You have to know when deceivers come so that that they will not shake you.

Some people will promise you the world. They will use the Word of God to compel you to do what they desire. Satan attempted this on the Son of God, Himself. It's almost humorous when you think of the audacity of Satan to attempt to use the *Word* against the Word, but he did. When Jesus had fasted forty days and nights and was led into the wilderness by the Holy Spirit (Mat. 4:1), Satan used Scripture to entice Jesus into disobedience.

> "If thou be the Son of God, cast thyself down: for it is written, He shall give his angels charge concerning thee: and in their hands they shall bear thee up, lest at any time thou dash thy foot against a stone (v.6)."

In 1 Kings 13, we read about an unknown prophet only referred to in the Word of God as "a man of God out of Judah." This prophet was given specific instruction by God to go and rebuke King Jeroboam and "cry against the altar." The prophet was told by God to leave Bethel in the opposite direction he came and was told specifically not to eat or drink in Bethel. The prophet was obedient for a moment, but on his way home, the word of his acts had gotten around town. An "old prophet in Bethel" wanted to have dinner with the man of God. At first the man of God refused, but then the old prophet lied saying "I am a prophet also as thou art; and an angel spake unto me by the word of the LORD, saying, Bring him back with thee into thine house, that he may eat bread and drink water" (1 King 13:18, KJV).

Evidently, this lying prophet knew the language. He could "talk the talk." If I can imagine the scene in our modern time, I would imagine the old prophet clasping his eyelids and frowning his face; clutching his arms and wagging his head back and forth as if the Spirit had moved upon him to declare this message. He was eloquent and articulate enough to cause this prophet who had heard so clearly from God to believe that God had somehow changed His mind.

The man of God heeded the words of the lying prophet. Ironically, after the old prophet deceived the man of God to eat and drink with him, the old prophet then turned around and prophesied to the man of God about how his rebellion had led him to certain doom. The very person who lied and tricked the man of God to disobey, turned around and wagged his religious finger at the man for being disobedient. After the man of God ate and went to return home, he was mauled to death by a lion. The lion wasn't even hungry because the Word tells us he just sat their with the donkey looking at the man of God.

Take heed to this passage of scripture. You have to watch what people are saying and how you respond to it because, "they lie in wait to deceive." When you are mature, you can hear what they say and you can understand how they say it. There are those who have tremendous eloquence and articulation but no substance and no facts to go along with it. You have to be careful so you won't fall into their traps. You must be mature enough to know that you are hearing something that does not coincide with the Word.

Jesus vs. The Man of God

Here, we witness two strong examples of what Satan is doing to the Body of Christ even now. We should never be so naïve as to think the enemy will not use the Word of God to deceive us. Notice the different responses from our two examples. Jesus, being mature in the Word, rejected the enemy by utilizing the Word of God. Jesus weighed every deception Satan presented with the Word of God. To be perfectly honest, everything Satan presented to Jesus was a practical request, but it wasn't part of God's will.

I believe Jesus could have turned the stones into bread with no problem. We witnessed Him turning water into wine. Jesus could have easily jumped off the mountain and simply walked on the air. We witnessed Him walk on water. And as much as we would like to deny this, Satan could have given Jesus earthly rule, because Satan is the Prince of the World.

Jesus recognized that all of those requests were carnal, temporal fixes that did not line up with God's will. A one time snack of bread transformed from stones would have filled Jesus' stomach, but would have food-poisoned His destiny. Proving His divinity by tempting God and jumping off of a cliff would have satisfied His ego, but would have plummeted His purpose to utter destruction. Lastly, accepting Satan's offer to rule the world would have given Jesus a little power, but He would have sacrificed *all power*, which has been given unto Him. For

70 to 80 years, a few knees would have bowed to Him, but because of His obedience, now "*every* knee shall bow, every tongue shall swear" (Isa. 45:23)Jesus is Lord .

Though I wish I could provide a long dissertation about the positives of the man of God, the fact is his disobedience gave him nothing but a blemish on the garment of history. Despite the fact that God used him in such a mighty way, and despite the fact that the man of God was faithful to God's word up until the old prophet lied about hearing from an angel, his story ended the moment he rebelled. Herein lies the drive behind Satan's ambition. Satan seeks to destroy the work and the very memory of God's people from the earth. Through deception and religiosity, the power of the Church is fading. We are finding it harder and harder to distinguish the lines that separate the righteous from unrighteous. All of the labor and sacrifices from the saints of old are being mauled by a satanic lion that has no other objective but to kill the Body.

So many people are spiritually abused by manipulative individuals who use the Word of God for personal gain. God wants the Body of Christ to be mature enough to distinguish a lie from the truth, even if it is wrapped in the pages of the Bible. So many Christians are destroyed by "lying old prophets in Bethel" who proclaim they have "a word from an angel." Take notice, the old prophet did not say he received a Word from the Lord; only a measly unknown angel. However the man of God *had* received his instructions directly from the Lord, God.

How many times have we received directions from God, Himself, only to allow someone to tell us that they have received word from a *lower* authority that we should do the opposite? Well, I have news for you. The Church is doing it everyday. We have been given direct instructions from God to win souls, to be a light in the darkness, but we allow the politicians to tell us that according to their authority, we can't preach against sin because it would be considered hate speech. We have been told to warn the world of sin and eternal damnation in hell, but we are allowing "old lying prophets in Bethel" to teach inclusivity. God is looking for a perfect, mature Church who can recognize the truth from lies, and He has given pastors, prophets, teachers, and evangelists to get the Body to this point of growth.

Maturation Through the Bible

In order to help the Body grow and mature, Word ministers will have to keep their heads and eyes in the Bible. I see preachers walking around with all kinds of books, but the question is: Where is the Bible? They have psychology books, sociology books, and finance books, all in an effort to share some kind of enlightenment with others, but they fall miserably short because they are not teaching the Bible. This is not to suggest we are not to read other books. Indeed we should read those books that line up with the Word of God to enhance the applicability of God's Word.

There are those who embrace the extreme that everything we need to know is in the Bible. I disagree because though our most important personage is the Spirit man, there are many practical, daily issues that we can learn through books. We must learn to embrace the information God has given to those whom He has equipped with knowledge and skill in our culture.

For example, the Bible has a lot to say about finances, but you can search all day long and you won't find any specific instructions on how to properly invest your money in the stock market. I'm sure you can find passages within the Word that reflect the benefit of a healthy diet, but you won't find anything in the Bible about the benefits of a brisk walk 30 minutes per day. This one habit would reduce the amount of individuals needing prayer and healing from cholesterol and blood pressure problems.

When it comes to the souls of man, the Bible is what we need. We must teach nothing more or less than the unadulterated word of God. Even while embracing the opinions of man that we find in books, we should never declare man's word over God's. Though we embrace the knowledge of saving money for a rainy day, we should never promote that earthly knowledge over God's word.

When the rich young ruler came to Jesus and asked "What must I do to have eternal life?" (Matt 19:16). Jesus said

"If thou wilt be perfect, go and sell that thou hast, and give to the poor, and thou shalt have treasure in heaven: and come and follow me" (Matt 19:21). You would be hard pressed to find such suggestions like this in books written by Donald Trump or Warren Buffet. Word ministers cannot preach the knowledge of the world to the souls of man. We must preach the Bible, and only the Bible.

What did Jesus teach? Jesus taught what His Father told Him to teach. He did not come up with some other subject matter; He could have because He had the power to do it, He had the knowledge to do it, He had the anointing to do it. He was anointed to preach before He left heaven, so He could have addressed a number of subjects from a myriad of angles. He could have made the people privy to new inventions that would have altered the course of commerce during His time, but because He was sent of God; because He was the delegated authority that God placed here on earth, He chose not to go against the teachings of His father.

Likewise, as Word ministers, we must approach our delegated authority to bring about maturity among Christians the same way Jesus did. We must preach and teach only what God tells us to preach and teach. This is not a time to invoke your own ideology. This is not a time to persuade people to think as you do. We must persuade people to think as Jesus thinks.

As a Bishop in the Church of God In Christ, I have often been asked why I don't preach a lot about C.O.G.I.C. doc-

trine. Why I am willing to preach at the church of another denomination? The reason is because I preach Christ only, not
denomination. I love the denomination of which I belong with
all of my heart, but I love my God more. I don't preach the ideology and interpretation of man—which is the root of denomi-
nationalism. God has one Word. The Word tells us there is but
"one Lord, one faith, one Baptism" (Eph. 4:5).

If we are going to mature, the Body of Christ must become stable. The Bible says we cannot be double-minded.
Christians of all denominations must stand together for "one
Lord" in "one Faith" under the one and only "Baptism" of the
Holy Ghost. As long as Christians are fighting amongst each
other about whether to worship on Saturdays or Sundays, we
will never address the needs of a dying world. Word ministers
waste countless hours teaching and defending the ideologies of
their denomination to the members of *their* church (who already belong to the denomination), when they should be
teaching the truths of God and the necessity of the Christian
body to go out and win souls.

Though such teaching will bring about rejection from
"church folks", this, too, is keeping with the mind of Jesus. Jesus came teaching God's truth, which vitiated the authority of
religious leaders and turned people's attention toward God and
away from man. As a result, He was "despised and rejected of
men; a man of sorrows, and acquainted with grief: and we hid
as it were our faces from him; he was despised, and we es-

teemed him not" (Isa. 53:3). He "came to his own and his own received him not" (John 1:11).

When we read that "he [Jesus] came to His own", to whom was the writer referring? Was he referring to Jesus' cousins, friends, and neighbors? No, the writer was referring to the so-called "saints"; the "church folks." Jesus went to the people who should have shared His conviction to lead people to God and those very people rejected Him. He stood there in the midst of controversy; but that did not stop His message to those who would receive Him, "to them gave He power to become the sons of God."

As we preach and teach, we must not worry about those who reject the teachings—those who refuse to grow. There is someone who wants to grow; who wants a better life; who wants to live a different life; who wants to go up in God; who wants to be "planted by the rivers of water, that bringeth forth his fruit in his season" (Ps. 1:3). What we have to do is teach them the Word — give them the Word of God.

When should we give them the Word? "Be instant in season and out of season" (2 Tim. 4:2); when it sounds right and when it doesn't sound right; when they pay tithe and when they don't pay tithe; when they pat you on the back and when they don't pat you on the back; when they say you preached a good message and when they sit down on you as if you said nothing at all. How should you preach? Under the anointing of God. How long should you preach? Until Jesus comes back. With what force should you preach? Under the anointing for it's the anointing that breaks the yoke. Speak the truth in love, so that we may grow up in Him.

Prepared for Presentation

When it all comes down to it, the true reason we are maturing is to be prepared for the Bridegroom—Jesus. He is coming back for His bride and He is not looking for a little, spoiled child with pig tails, and mud all over her dress. This is not the kind of bride the Father wants for His only begotten Son. As we grow spiritually, we are growing up in Him. We are becoming more like Him and becoming more intimate with Jesus. So the reason you are maturing is so we can be properly presented.

In days when parents betrothed their children, no father would take his six-year-old girl and present her to a bridegroom. He had to wait until that girl matured. Although that girl got older and developed physically, she was yet not mature. When that child reached maturity, then that father could say to that bridegroom or that intended, "I will give you my blessings and present to you my daughter for matrimony."

Likewise, a lot of people in the Church look mature. They have the physical attributes of a mature Christian. They pronounce blessings on every person who speaks to them. They shake and quake whenever the church is in high praise. They wear their dresses down to the ground and wear panty hose with sandals, but within, they are still little babies in their spirits.

If we are going to be presented before our Father to be a bride to the bridegroom, the Church as a whole must grow and mature. The growth of the Church must begin with you.

CHAPTER 2
CHRISTLIKENESS

Growth is most likely to occur when we focus our attention on one area at a time. The most basic of these is Salvation. Without spiritual life, which can only be found through the birth of the spiritual man, spiritual growth is impossible. We say "spiritual life"—not spiritual activity. Many people confuse the two. Being able to run the aisles of the sanctuary, and sound spiritually deep does not equate to walking a "spiritual life."

Spiritual life is comprehensive, encompassing; it is not fragmented but is the totality of you. Who you are is directly linked to your spiritual walk. When the Scripture makes reference to "you" in the Bible, it has reference to your spirit and not your flesh. When Jesus said, "you" must be born again, certainly He was not talking about your flesh. Nicodemus prudently asked the question, "How can a man be born when he is old? can he enter the second time into his mother's womb, and be born?" (John 3:4). Jesus responded. "Verily, verily, I say unto thee, Except a man be born of water and of the Spirit, he cannot enter into the kingdom of God" (v. 5).

Therefore, we have to have spiritual life in order to have spiritual growth. A new believer's position is perfect in Christ. However, his or her daily practice is far from it. When we come to Christ we have already been justified, we are sanctified in the Word, therefore, in Christ you are perfect. In terms of your daily practice and activities, we are not perfect. Herein lies the waging inward battle that all Christians face. We feel that in our daily practice we are perfect, but we are constantly battling negative and carnal thoughts that come into our minds.

We wonder why we behave in the manner in which we do, and why we do what we do. As Paul states "For the good that I would I do not: but the evil which I would not, that I do" (Rom. 7:19). Paul goes on to explain why we behave in this manner. "Now if I do that I would not, it is no more I that do it, but sin that dwelleth in me" (v.20). Now how is it that Paul can say "it is no more I that do it"? Is Paul exculpating himself? Is he schizophrenic? No, Paul realizes that as a born-again Christian, He—the true Paul who is the spirit of Paul—is not a sinner. However, because Paul is a triune being, and 1/3 of his being is flesh, he is constantly torn and in battle with this fleshly side.

Romans 6:12 teaches us "let not sin reign in your mortal bodies that ye should obey it in the lust thereof." This indicates sin is always present. Because you have flesh, you have sin. However, you must not let it reign; don't let it have control. You are responsible for the control, you are responsible for your behavior, your attitude, and your disposition. If you allow a specific sin to reign in your body, then you become a "sinner." As a Christian, though you may sin, you are not a sinner.

I teach my congregation against the old—albeit foolish—sentiment promulgated by saints who claim, "I'm just a sinner saved by grace." I teach them that when we accept Christ, we are no longer sinners, but have been given "power to become sons of God" (John 1:12). We are "joint heirs with Jesus Christ" (Rom. 8:17). Sinners practice a lifestyle of sin. Christians do not practice this lifestyle. We are constantly perfecting our lifestyles to fall in line with the will of God. Although our daily practice will not always be perfect; we learn and we grow.

B.I.B.L.E: Basic Instructions Before Leaving Earth

We've all heard of the acronym attributed to the Bible: Basic Instructions Before Leaving Earth. Although this may seem cliché, the acronym could not be more perfect. Our understanding of the teachings of the Bible must grow if we are to become perfect. We must understand these basic instructions if we are to become perfect, which is the contingency for Christ's coming. As we discussed in Chapter 1, Jesus is not coming back for an imperfect bride. Don't go to Bible study and weekly church service, constantly receiving and never growing. Hearing the Word is always good, but just hearing a preacher or teacher talk about things they learned from the Bible will only take us so far. If we are going to grow in Christlikeness, we have to make a conscious effort to exercise our spirits in the Word and cause them to grow. To do this, we must saturate our spirits to the extent that the subject matter becomes a part of us.

Growth is taking that which is taught and allowing it to dwell in you so the explosiveness that results from it is a part of you and does not leave you. That's what God meant when He told Joshua not to let the Words depart from his mouth. God was not forbidding Joshua to speak the Words, but instead commanding him to make the Word of God the primary thing he speaks. In other words, keep them as a part of your inner person.

Not only are we to fill ourselves with the Word, but we must also exercise the Word. There's nothing more satisfying to a mother than to see her newborn child eating with a healthy appetite. If that baby has not begun to exercise her legs, flail her arms around, try to stand or turn, after one month, that mother will become concerned. Yes, the baby is eating fine, but the baby is not using the muscles for which the food is supposed to supply strength. If this baby continues to eat only, but never exercise, the very food that should provide nutrition and strength will begin to harm that child.

In the Church, we are becoming very comfortable with being the baby that feeds all day. We fill up on the Word of God and become bloated with the Holy Ghost. Then we go home, flop down in front of the television to watch the football game and do nothing with that "food". We go to work and flop down in front of the computer and do nothing with our spiritual muscles. And though we are fed well, we are spiritually fat and complacent, and our growth is retarded.

Our consistent application of the teachings must increase. As we learn, we must exercise those things which we are taught. We must ask ourselves "What is it that I have been taught and how do I apply these things?" Don't learn for the sake of knowledge; learn for the sake of doing. I can recall as a young preacher, reading my Bible preparing for the sermon I was to preach, when God spoke to my spirit. "What are you doing Jerry?" The question was odd to me, and being who God made me, I spoke frankly with the Lord; "Lord, you know what I'm doing, I'm studying for this week's sermon." Then God spoke to my spirit and said, "Stop studying to preach and start studying to live."

In essence, I was studying for the test. I was putting together topics and quotes to deliver an eloquent speech, but God wants us to know Him for ourselves. More than being a good preacher, God wanted and wants me to be a good Christian. Likewise, more than just being good church attendees, God wants us to be good Christians. He's not interested in us simply hearing the Word, He is more interested in us *doing* the Word.

Being a good student of the Word for the purpose of telling others about it does not prepare you for godly service. I can remember a young lady I went to school with from junior high all the way through four years of college. We graduated at the same time. My classmate never made less than a B+ and she wept sorely when she received the B+ because it did not meet her high expectation of an A+. She was a consummate student of her chosen field of expertise and she knew everything about it.

After college, she immediately became a teacher. Strapped with a ton of book knowledge she was prepared to share with her students the wealth of years of study. However, she quickly came to the conclusion that she could not handle teaching children. Why? My classmate had the letter but she did not know how to deal with children who behaved un-seemly. She had the letter, but she did not know how to do anything but teach the subject matter that she was taught.

There is more to teaching than simple recitation of in-formation. You have to have control of your class, you have to deal with the daily emotional and spiritual issues that your students are facing. You have to recognize and work with the var-ied learning styles of each student. That aspiring educator quit teaching after her first year. She could not handle it. She was not prepared. Although she was a brain with a wealth of accu-mulated knowledge, she did not know how to apply those teachings in the real world.

We know that "faith cometh by hearing" (Rom. 10:17), but "as the body without the spirit is dead, so faith without works is dead" (James 2:20). We can "hear" the Word to obtain faith, but the consistency in applying those teachings must increase. We must learn and do something each day with that which we have been taught. We must apply the teachings and stop being despondent and ill-informed. So many people know scriptures but don't know how to use them.

When the devil came to temp Jesus, Jesus used the power of the Word. Every area in which the devil tempted Jesus, Jesus used the Word. We need to learn to give the Word in every area of our tests. Whenever we are being tried, give Word. Stop using philosophy; the spirit realm is not moved by philosophy. Evil spirits don't tremble at the name of Plato or Socrates. Demons are not cast out by the philosophies of Aristotle. Bodies are not healed by the word of Freud. The only power to change our lives is found in the word of God.

People need to know that we know the WORD, not in terms of our discourse, but in terms of our behavior. Some of us want to give a dissertation. We want to impress the world with big theological words and show off our deep exegesis of passage. When the dust clears, we find nothing more than a dusty, empty cup with no lifesaving water to share.

I can remember listening to a preacher who came to the National C.O.G.I.C. Convocation in Memphis, TN. The preacher from New York thought he was in a college room, evidently and began to give a lecture. You don't give lectures in Memphis. When they put you up to preach, you preach. He began to lecture about the different degrees of love. He condescendingly ranted about how ignorant we were about love. Before long, the Presiding Bishop put a note on the lectern that told him to sit down.

This preacher evidently felt he had a degree of knowledge and wanted everyone else to know how much more he knew than them. Instead, he should have learned to "share" his new understanding with others. When you are a mature Christian, you apply the Word by learning to share. Others are going through just like you are, so learn how to share those things that you know. Don't hoard your knowledge.

I am reminded of the women of my neighborhood when I was growing up in South Bend, Indiana. When these women learned to cook or bake certain foods, they would share their recipes. They wanted others to know how to cook the foods that they enjoyed. They found joy in sharing the same pleasures they had experienced with their neighbors. They wanted others to know the same joy. David reflected this same mentality when he wrote "O taste and see that the LORD is good" (Ps. 34:8). David had experienced a food beyond compare—the Bread of Life— and he wanted to share it with the world. We, too, should share the Word of God freely and humbly.

People need to see the application of God's Word in your life, and the most powerful way you can show people the Word is to *apply* the Word. Share with others through your actions how good God has been to you. That's what Paul did with Agrippa. He talked about the experience that he had on his way to Damascus and how he became saved. He shared that story with King Agrippa. That story alone would have been useless had it not been for the new behavior that Paul displayed. Paul went from persecuting Christians to applying the Word and being one of the most outspoken Christians. As a result of Paul's application, even King Agrippa said "thou almost persuaded me to be a Christian" (Act 26:28).

CHAPTER 3

Maturity Concerning Events in our Lives

Christian maturity helps us to deal with life—plain and simple. There are times when we have problems within our lives and we try to use our faith as a get-out-of-trouble-free card. We act like spoiled spiritual babies and think that because we are Christians, God is going to make all of the boogie men go away. This is not realistic.

We need to have maturity in relation to the events of life. There are events with which we are confronted and we need to be able to face them head on. We won't be able to side-step them or dodge them. Too many people are dodging responsibilities and acting as if all things are well when they are not. It is a mature person who understands that there are problems. More specifically, you are mature when you not only understand that there are problems, but strategize the solution to the problem.

If you have a problem and you are not moving quickly toward its solution, then you are not mature. As a matter of fact, a person who is irresponsible has not matured at all. Maturity brings about responsibility. As Christians, we need to learn how to handle the most difficult times of our lives. There are different circumstances and every day is not the same. As soon as you are able to get over one hurdle, there is yet another. When you swim across one river, there is another. And when you tunnel through one mountain there is another. Life is filled, as the song says, "with swift transitions." and you need to prepare yourself for them.

We say "every day is the same with Jesus," which is true because He does not deviate from His posture. However, your life and the changes within your life are different from day to day and you need to focus on how to face life realistically. To do this you must have a mind of sanity, Proverbs 4:23 states, "Keep thine heart with all diligence for out of it are the issues of life."

The writer is not writing about cardiovascular health in this passage. He is writing about your spirit. Keep thy "spirit" with all diligence for out of your "spirit" are the issues of life. Issues don't come from your flesh, they come from your spirit. Wherever you are is contingent upon your spirit person. If you are weak in spirit, you will be weak in life. When you are strong in spirit, you will be strong in life. Do everything within your ability to keep your sanity by keeping your spirit. Out of your inner person come the things that you do, say, and think.

When you act out of sorts, it's not because of what another person has done to you. It is because of who you are in-
side. Napoleon Hill, one of the most successful men in America, whose writing inspired such individuals as Mahatma
Ghandi, said in a lecture that he felt that he had so learned to
control his inner man that if a person walked up and slapped
him in the face, that he (Hill) would most likely "pity" the man
than be angry with him. Hill said he would pity that man because that man has so little inner peace and control. He went
on to say that a person should "never be so weak as to let another person cause him or her to become vengeful." Hill is giving the same instruction that the aforementioned scripture is
teaching—"Keep yourself."

God has given you complete and utter control over one
thing—yourself. You can't control any person's or animal's actions. You can't control anything on this earth but your own
behavior. You can control the thoughts that come into your
mind by bringing them under subjection to the Word of God,
and you can control your actions with a simple choice. You
need to keep yourself so that irrespective of what comes your
way, negative or the positive, you can handle the events of
your life.

Listen to God

How then can we keep our hearts? In the 4th Chapter of Proverbs, Solomon writes "My son, attend unto my words, incline thine ear unto my sayings." Let's focus on these words. **"Attend"**, meaning to give attention to; let **"my words"** be significant; give attention to my words and incline thine ear unto my sayings. Don't listen to what everybody else says, as we often do, but listen to what God says. We love to listen to each other. The Lord will speak to us about a certain situation and then we will go meandering through the neighborhood or the church trying to find someone who has yet another message. God wants us to listen to His instructions and understand how He will handle situations, so that we may handle our situations in similitude.

When the Lord speaks, you don't need another message, you don't need a greater understanding, or a different understanding —what you need to do is "incline thine ear" unto His sayings and attend unto His words, then be a doer of His word. Doing His word will help you through the storms of your life. When you have His words and listen to His sayings, you can look at life realistically.

"Looking at life realistically" means seeing life according to facts—not emotions, biases, or prejudices. For instance, if a man loses a job, he may be quick to claim that he lost his job due to some type of injustice. In some cases, it may be true, but in other cases it may not be. This person would do himself an injustice to play the victim card and look at the situation through the lens of his emotions. Instead, he should seek God's opinion and get the facts from the Creators perspective. One thing I have found is that God never beats around the bush. He gives it to you straight. After seeking God's perspective, that worker may find out that "realistically" he was a poor worker or that God is freeing him up for another job.

In cases where it seems like all of the terrors of life have unleashed on you, many times we make the mistake of blaming God. We believe God has turned against us. This unrealistic, non-factual view of the situation will cause us to stray from God, leading us directly where the enemy wants us to be. When we view the situations realistically, we know adversity doesn't come our way independent of the force of Satan and his demons. It is the will of Satan to destroy you, not God's. God asked, "Have I any pleasure at all that the wicked should die... and not that he should return from his ways and live?" (Ezekiel 18:23).

Jesus told Peter and the disciples, "Satan desireth to sift you as wheat, but I pray God that your faith fails you not" (Luke 22:31). It is Satan's goal to destroy you and to sift you as wheat. That's his mission. When you are within the word of God, you understand who your true enemy is. It's not your neighbor, brother, sister, or co-worker. It's the force of Satan using those people as instruments. The battle is not between you and people. The battle is not even between you and Satan. The battle is between God and Satan.

We learned this in the Book of Job. Satan didn't attack Job because he had a grudge with Job. In fact, Satan wasn't even thinking about attacking Job because he considered Job beyond reach. Satan said, "Hast not thou made a hedge about him?" (Job 1:10). The trials of Job's came about as a result of God's desire to prove to Satan how strong He was in Job's life.

You carry God's Spirit so that brings you into the battle. However, you don't have to fight because it's God's battle. You never have to fight God's battle. All God requires you to do is listen and do what He tells you to do. In 2 Chronicles 20:16 God told King Jehoshaphat exactly what to do.

> "To morrow go ye down against them: behold, they come up by the cliff of Ziz; and ye shall find them at the end of the brook, before the wilderness of Jeruel."

The instructions were simple and the task was easy. Jehoshaphat listened to God, and when God's people marched to war they found their foes already destroyed. Not only did they not have to fight, but for their inconvenience of having to walk to the battlefield,

> "they found among them in abundance both riches with the dead bodies, and precious jewels,

which they stripped off for themselves, more than they could carry away: and they were three days in gathering of the spoil, it was so much" (v. 25).

When you incline your ear to His sayings, you know what the end results are going to be. We are not walking through life blindfolded. God does not give us a roadmap for life, but He has clearly shown us our destination. All He wants us to do is just live by faith. The Word states the "Just shall live by faith" (Heb. 10:38). It did not say the just shall live by blindness. You should know where you are going even though you are going by faith.

Jesus knew He was going to the Cross. Paul knew he was going to face Nero's chopping block. John knew he was going to the isle of Patmos, but they lived by faith. Likewise, you should know where you're going. You may not know every nook and cranny of the voyage, but all God wants you to do is walk in obedience, and allow the Word of God to lead you. David said, "the Lord is my shepherd, I shall not want... yea, though I walk through the valley of the shadow of death I will fear no evil for thou art with me..." (Psalm 23). You may be headed for the valley, but it's alright because you are with God as you go. Just listen to God.

Acknowledge God

Proverbs 3:6-- In all thy ways acknowledge Him and He shall direct thy paths.

So many times, we run and make decisions and after we get in a mess we ask God to help us out of it. However, God tells us clearly in His word to acknowledge Him. As a pastor and Bishop, I notice that sometimes people confuse this scripture and think it means to go and ask the Pastor before they make a decision. Don't acknowledge the pastor, acknowledge God. If I have the answers to your questions or the solution to your problem, then when you acknowledge God, He will inform you that Jerry Maynard has your answer. Don't run to a man first— acknowledge God and He will inform you where your answer is.

There is only so much help that I can give. I remember one day I had 37 consultations. I felt like Moses when he was judging all the issues of the children of Israel. Now, I'll be honest, a human being can only do so much. Carrying the burdens of that many people in one day will wear any finite human down. There are only so many answers that I can give; only so much wisdom I have and advice I can give. After a while, I'll be going around in circles. I'll confuse one answer with another, one problem with another and that person will fail to get the help they need.

God will tell you where your solution is and He will help you through what you are going through. This is what

God does. Every single voice and problem that comes God's way is distinct and unique. He hears and understands you so that when you call, He does not confuse you with anybody else, nor does He confuse your circumstances or the manner in which He has to deliver you.

Acknowledge God in all thy ways. Before you get married; before you get a divorce, before you separate, before you date, before you take a job; before you buy a car, a house; before you buy that Rolex — acknowledge Him.

Why should we acknowledge Him? We acknowledge Him because He knows what's down the road; He knows whether or not you have what it takes to pay for whatever you are buying. He knows whether or not that person you think looks so good is just putting on a front. Everybody can show their best side for a little while, but He knows the real person. I spoke to a brother who told a young lady before they were married that he "loved her to death." After they got married she treated him so badly, he said he wished he could love her *to death*. God will help you so that you don't have to come to those kinds of resolves. He has somebody compatible for you; He has the right house, the right job, the right position, and the right school.

Some people have paid and owe a lot of money for school, and when they graduated, they couldn't find a job. They should have asked God before they took the course. God knows the ability that He has given to each person. He knows what a person can endure; He knows what a person can bear, therefore, acknowledge Him and He will have direct you to the right place.

Rejoice in Your Suffering

Now, when you do go through and the enemy is wreaking havoc in your life and heaping coals of fire upon your head, there is a posture that you must assume to get him off of you: you must learn how to rejoice in your suffering; Matthew 5:12 states,

> "blessed are ye when men shall revile you and persecute you and say all manner of evil against you falsely for my sake. Rejoice, and be exceeding glad for great is your reward in heaven; for so persecuted they the prophets which were before you."

When you know you have done what God has instructed and you know you have kept your heart with all diligence, you can rejoice when you are persecuted. Notice, Jesus qualified His statement at the end with "for my name's sake." If you are being persecuted because you are a gossiper, you can't look to God for any assistance. That persecution will not be counted as righteousness to you.

Maybe you have not had that experience but sometimes it looks like the devil is coming from everywhere. However, in the midst of the storm and uneasiness, in the trying of your times; you can rejoice and be exceeding glad. Every once in a while when the devil wants you to go into a stupor, you can say to him, "Not so! Far too many times have I cried unto the Lord and He has heard my cry; too many times have I depended upon Him and He was always there; too often have I trusted in Him and He has never failed me, and the song says 'He's never failed me yet, never failed me yet— Jesus Christ has never failed me yet; everywhere I go I want the world to know that Jesus Christ has never failed me yet.'"

When you mature in the Lord, you are not regularly discouraged nor are you anxious on a regular basis. The reason is because God will take what they meant for your bad and turn it into your good. When we mature in Christ, we can handle the difficult events of our lives. We can lean on the words of the Apostle Paul who said, "all things, work together for the good of them who are called according to His will" (Rom. 8:28). If God loves you and if you love God, things will work together for your good.

CHAPTER 4

Maturity Over Things

We are living in the time wherein we need to be able to divorce ourselves from "things." Though this word is so very general, it is also, very destructive. Things will ruin your life — equally, they will run your life. When you grow in maturity, things don't dictate to you, you dictate to things. You determine what it is — and what it is not. Spend your money for what you want. The only obligation you have is to pay your tithe and give your offering and what you do with the rest of your money is your business. You can burn it if you want, but don't love the burning of it. Whatever car you want, get it but don't love it. If you want a Rolls Royce go and get one but don't get three jobs to pay for it because then you can't give proper service, worship, and praise to God.

The world passes away and the lust thereof, but he that doeth the will of God abideth forever. Things pass away. Try going a year without paying your bills and see what happens. The world gets caught up in things, but we need to get caught up in God. God is more precious to us than anything. We need to have proper usage of things. Galatians lets us know we need to be temperate in all things. There is one method by which we know that we will remain that way—that is if we live in the Spirit.

When you set your goals on things, you will never be satisfied. No matter what you have you will always want something bigger and better. If you have a job making $50,000 a year and hear that another is making $60,000, you will want that job; no matter how long you've been on the $50,000 job. Once you get the $60,000 job, you'll want the $70,000. You can never be satisfied with things. That is why we find ourselves moping from time to time trying to find the answer. We stay up all night tossing and turning because we are not satisfied. We need to get our minds off of things and get them on God.

We have to make sure that we don't allow our lust for things to take precedent over what God calls us to do. Many times, when God calls for us to give to the Church or to others, we are so preoccupied in the things that we want to do, often we are unable to do the things that God requires us to do. When we speak with regard to Christian maturity we must learn to maintain proper priorities.

John 2:15 states: "Love not the world, neither the things that are in the world. If any man love the world, the love of the Father is not in him." That seems to indicate that somewhere there needs to be a separation between you and the world. Physically, it is impossible for you to separate yourself from the world because you live in the world. You interact with people of the world and have relationships. However, you don't have to love it. Jesus said,

> "If ye were of the world, the world would love its own. But because you are not of the world, but I have chosen you out of the world, therefore, the world hateth you," (John 15:9)

It's amazing how hard we try to be a part of something that hates us. So many Christians are struggling to be accepted in a world that innately rejects them. When you come to God, your living standards change, and the people in the world don't agree with your choice. If you chose to walk around with tattoos all over your body and earring piercing hanging all over your face, the world would say that you were "expressing yourself." If you chose to party all weekend and sleep around, they would call you a "bachelor." If you chose to be Muslim, Buddhist, or even Wicca, the world would respect your religious freedom. However, the moment you choose to serve Christ, you become an outcast.

Now why is that? It's not because of your flesh that they don't agree. It's because of your Spirit. It's because there is a positive identification between you and the Lord, and Satan does not want anyone to stop him from being their boss. He gets upset when he cannot control you. He knows he can't get you to turn back to blatantly sinning, but if he can get you to focus on the things of the world, he can entice you back to him.

Having Money vs. Loving Money

I understand that many of us have a misconception of money and we say that if you are rich you will not be able to enter into the Kingdom of God because of Jesus' statement that "it is easier for a camel to go through the eye of a needle, than for a rich man to enter into the kingdom of God" (Matt 19:24). First of all, Jesus was not talking about a sewing needle. We know that there was a passage in the Jerusalem Wall called the "Eye of a Needle" where the camels were brought into the city. When the camels would come, they would be so overly packed with bundles of goods, that when they would got ready to go to Jerusalem those camels would have to get down on their knees and crawl through.

The significance of that statement is that the camels would have to get low enough to get through. Likewise, the rich man will have to humble himself and get low in order to enter the Kingdom of Heaven. That's why Jesus told the rich young ruler to sell all he owned. Jesus knew the young man's life was caught up in his "things." When we put our "things" before God, we are not walking in humility but instead magnifying our wealth above God.

This does not mean that rich people cannot make it to heaven. Rich people can, but they must humble themselves and not love the things that they have more than they love God. It is okay to enjoy things. Get what you want; enjoy what you want; but don't love things to the extent that you become a slave to them.

Hear No Evil, See No Evil

You can control your attraction to things by controlling what you listen to and what you watch. As mature Christians, we should not watch some of the movies and listen to some of the music we listen to. We should not be consumed with so many idol things. Some of these movies permeate your mind. Many single people struggle with the "gift" of singleness because they keep feeding themselves with music, movies, and books that are focused on romance, and in most cases, lust.

I am not saying there is anything wrong with romance, and I don't call singleness a "gift" out of a sense of regret. Both marriage and singleness are a gift from God. As Paul said to the Corinthians about marriage: "Every man hath his proper GIFT of God" (1 Cor. 7:7). Solomon tells us that "whoso findeth a wife, findeth a good thing, and obtaineth favor of the Lord" (Prov. 18:22); and Paul explained,

"There is difference also between a wife and a virgin. The unmarried woman careth for the things of the Lord, that she may be holy both in body and in spirit: but she that is married careth for the things of the world, how she may please her husband" (1 Cor: 7:34).

However, we find that the single people are doing what Paul said the married people would be doing: "caring for the things of the world." When you fill your spirit with the lyrics of songs, and read the books, and watch the adult rated movies you will eventually begin acting out what you're hearing, seeing, and reading. This is a natural law. According to the Bible, "As he thinketh in his heart, so is he" (Prov. 23:7). If you think on the things of the world on a regular basis, then you will inevitably fulfill your worldly desires. You can control your desire for things by meditating on the things of God more than the things of the world.

5

Points of Christian Maturity

CHAPTER 5

Love

There are five points of maturity that I feel are necessary for every Christian. I believe that if we can mature in these areas, we will find ourselves more effective and happy Christians. First and foremost is maturing in love! It takes maturity to love. I'm not talking about the infatuation we have when we meet a beautiful person for the first time; but a love that looks beyond all faults.

This is the way we have to love each other in the Church. We have to love not for what we can get out of our fellow saints, but because the Spirit of God has made a deposit within that person's Spirit. When you love like this, you are actually loving God. When God's Spirit lives within you, you can identify with other people even if they have problems.

The Bible states, "charity [love] shall cover the multitude of sins" (1 Pet. 4:8), and although you may not appreciate someone personally, you love them in the Spirit. Love anchors us into a position wherein we are able to hold the status quo in love until changes are made. In your own home, you may have some unpleasant situations, but love keeps you until changes come. Sometimes, when you love a person, you don't even mention what they have done to offend you; you just love them and forgive them.

I remember one of the speakers at a marriage seminar we hosted at my church gave his testimony of repeated infidelity. He told us how his wife was praying for his salvation and how she loved him so much that she refused to leave him. He explained how after giving his heart to the Lord, he felt the need to repent to his wife and confess all of his infidelities. He went to his wife with tears in his eyes and sat her down. "Sweetheart, I have to tell you something." Before he could continue, his wife told him that she already knew everything he was going to tell her and that she had forgiven him a long time ago.

I'm not one to tell a person to stay in a relationship where a spouse is perpetually unfaithful, but I'm not going to tell a person to leave a perpetually unfaithful spouse either. Let's not forget about Hosea, whom God commanded to marry, and remain married to a prostitute. I believe that you must follow the unction of the Spirit in such cases. The power of this story is that before this man was willing to repent, his wife had already forgiven him. More amazing is the fact that she never told him that she knew about his indiscretions. Many of us are holding on to anger from years ago only because the person has not ask for forgiveness.

Even though the offense is often minor and could have easily been released, we're still holding on to it, just waiting for that person to ask "will you forgive me?" When we mature in love, we learn to release offenses and forgive without coercion. If you walk in the unity of the Spirit, and if you love somebody, you will want to understand them.

When you love, you put yourself in the place of your fellow man. You consider another's plight as if you were in the same situation. The Scripture tells us "If your brother be overtaken in a fault, ye who are spiritual restore such a one in the spirit of meekness, considering thyself, lest ye also be tempted"(Gal 6:1).

CHAPTER 6

Humility

What is humility? Is it walking around with your head hung low and shirking any resemblance of confidence? To the contrary, humility is really an act of strength, not timidity. Humility is understanding the power of who you are and of who God made you, but also understanding that power in connection with God's plan. Humility is taking no credit for your strengths, knowing that if it were not for God, you would have nothing. When David reigned as king of Israel, the nation was mighty and powerful. They conquered all of their enemies. However, the psalmist wrote in response to the nation's power, "If it had not been for the Lord who was on our side..." (Psa: 124, KJV).

Not only is humility a soberness of thought, but it is also an act of submission. As mature Christians, we must learn to submit to God and His will. At times, this can be the most difficult thing to do. It is hard to walk a road with no roadmap. My good friend Donnie McClurkin sang, "What do you do, when you've done all you can; seems like it's never enough."

There are times when God tells you to do a certain thing and you will give it your all, only to come upon what seems like failure. This is confusing and extremely frustrating. However, when we humble ourselves or submit ourselves to God's perfect will, we are able to endure the challenges of the call.

When we humble ourselves to God's will, we are able to be used. We can be effective vessels for the Kingdom. Like Abraham, we, too, will be willing to walk into the midst of nowhere with nothing more than a promise from God that He will provide. When we allow our pride to set in, we refuse to give God one hundred percent of our lives because we are afraid of failure.

You know there are things you have not done because you are wondering "what if it doesn't work?" When will we realize that we don't have to defend God? We don't have to prove God is powerful to the world. God is able to do that all by Himself. When Elijah challenged the prophets of Ba'al, he didn't do anything but ask God to prove Himself. Unlike the prophets of Ba'al, Elijah didn't go through any ceremonial exercises. He didn't cut his skin, perform any sacred incantations, or sing any special songs. Instead he simply spoke,

> "Hear me, O LORD, hear me, that this people may know that thou art the LORD God, and that thou hast turned their heart back again" (1 King 18:37).

After that simple prayer, God did above and beyond what was needed. When we walk in humility, we learn to let God be God. We learn that "all things work together" when God's plan is in progress.

Many times we give up on God's plan because our pride won't allow us to look beyond what seem like failures. If we would humble ourselves to God's omnipotence; if we would surrender and submit to God's total plan, we would find out those roadblocks and pitfalls are not failures at all, but merely the natural labyrinth leading to God's ultimate plan.

CHAPTER 7

Gratefulness

The next point of maturity is learning how to be grateful. Motivational speaker Brian Tracy says that he discovered that he could travel the world over with ease by using two simple phrases; "Please" and "Thank you." He explained how people with whom he travelled had more problems and were often treated worse because of their own lack of gratitude and appreciation to the inhabitants of the various locations.

We must learn to be grateful to God and man. I know this is a Christian book, so you may be looking for some deep thesis on spiritual gratefulness, but we fail to realize that being grateful to your neighbor is a profoundly powerful tool in Christian maturity. Just saying "thank you for what you have done for me" is a spiritual exercise.

Gratefulness is, in actuality, a manifestation of humility. Have you ever given a gift to an ungrateful person? If you have, then you know that person had an arrogant sense of entitlement so they didn't feel they should have to show appreciation for anything. After an encounter like that, you most likely will make up your mind that you won't be doing another thing for that person if you can help it. If he or she were on fire, you probably wouldn't waste a .99 cent bottle of water to put the fire out. This is the same impression we leave about the Body of Christ when we don't show appreciation.

Don't take people for granted. The world—although it denounces everything we stand for—still holds us to the standards we profess. When we show gratefulness, we draw others to us. People become excited about being in our presence and more importantly, are excited about who we are and what we are about. They are excited because our grateful attitudes make them feel better about themselves. Showing sincere gratitude lets people know that they have done something that is special and worthy of appreciation. Showing gratitude makes people feel important. People love to share time with people who make them feel important.

When we show ungratefulness and arrogance, we demonstrate a behavior that pushes people away. No one wants to do anything or even remotely imitate the lifestyle of an ungrateful person. As Christians, we are called to be a light in the darkness. Light exposes things, and hopefully it will expose that which is good.

As well as man, be grateful to God. Be grateful to God in the good times and the bad times. It is so easy to thank God when good things happen to us, but we are hard pressed to thank God when situations are not in our favor. When we get a new car or a new house, we say "God has been good to me!"

But before you got the new car or the new house, God had been good to you. When you were living in a two bedroom apartment with three children, God was good to you. When you were riding the bus to work, God was good to you.

A spirit of gratitude is a lifestyle that looks beyond circumstances and sees the big picture. Gratefulness understands what is precious and important in life. Health, strength, and inner peace can keep you far greater than money, new cars and fancy houses.

We've all heard about the man who complained daily about his old, worn-out shoes until he saw a man with no feet. This man with old shoes was so upset that he could not get new shoes, but never stopped to thank God for the shoes he had, or for the feet to walk. We must take to heart that these are benefits of God's grace and mercy. The standard amenities of life are not requirements.

When we are going through the trials of life, we often think we are alone in our struggles, but there is somebody whose situation is worse than yours. Christians have to learn how to be grateful—grateful and then patient.

CHAPTER 8

PATIENCE

When it comes to patience, many people immediately think about those pesky neighbors or co-workers who get on their "last nerves." These people cause our blood to boil and we pray for—PATIENCE! Yes, this is a form of patience that is essential in the life of a mature Christian, noted in 1 Thess. 5:14; "Now we exhort you, brethren... be patient toward all men." However, if you really stop to study the patience emphasized in the Word, you will find that patience is not an aesthetically pleasing garment of temperament that makes us more amicable to others, but instead, patience is spiritual armor. Patience is a tool in confrontation and combat, not a blanket for picnics and times of peace.

Jesus described the importance of patience best in Luke 21:19 when He instructed the disciples "in your patience possess ye your souls." For 13 verses preceding this statement, Jesus gave His famous "the days will come" speech, where He tells of all of the evils that will befall the Earth. He told the disciples of "wars and commotions (v.9)"; how "nations shall rise against nations (v.10)"; of earthquakes, famines, pestilence, fearful sights and signs from heaven (v.11)"; and how men would "lay their hands on you, and persecute you, delivering you up to the synagogues, and into prisons, being brought before kings and rulers" for His name's sake.

After describing all these intimidating events, Jesus did not tell the disciples to go learn karate or to go make swords. He didn't tell them to go dig bunkers to prepare for war. Instead, Jesus told them to possess their souls in "patience". This should shed an entirely new light on the power of this spiritual fruit. Patience is not about making you nice—although being nice is a bi-product of spiritual maturity. Patience is not about waiting at a red light quietly. Patience is spiritual body armor for a time of trial and tribulation.

Paul said it clearly when he explained that we "glory in tribulations also; knowing that tribulations worketh patience; and patience, experience, and experience hope" (Rom. 5:3). Of the 33 times the word "patience" is mentioned in the New Testament, you will find a good majority of those instances are preceded by some mention of trials, tribulations, or long suffering.

The fact is, as Christians, we are in a spiritual war. The Word of God prepares us for this spiritual war, just as every aspect of a soldier's life is preparing him for possible combat. From the regimented schedule and detail-oriented bed straightening, to the physical training and war simulations. There is nothing a soldier will experience in boot camp that is simply day-to-day living. Likewise, there is nothing in the Word of God that just happened to be written. Every Word is powerful, and this ideal of patience is also a tool of combat. As mature Christians, we must understand this. We must understand the importance of patience in its most critical interpretation. Patience is the armor in which you must possess your soul.

So the question is: "What is patience and how do I use it?" Patience—contrary to popular belief—is not passivity. Patience is not a state of being, but quite the opposite, it is an action. People don't possess patience, people practice patience; they execute it. Why is this knowledge important? It is important for you—a maturing Christian—to understand this because it alleviates any excuses for not utilizing this tool. It's easy to claim that you are not patient when you believe it is an inbred attribute, but when you understand that you have the power to exercise patience, you then must come to grips with the fact that you are refusing to be patient.

Patience does not exempt you from the feelings of frustration, anger, fear, or pain. In fact, without these dynamics, we would not need patience at all. The very definition of patience is *"bearing of provocation, annoyance, misfortune, or pain, without complaint, loss of temper, irritation, or the like."* Patience is a deliberate act to endure a situation with a positive attitude.

When we say the word "positive," we should adjust our interpretation of that word from the ideas of fun-loving laughter and frolicking. Instead, we should apply an interpretation of forward movement, progress. Hardships and setbacks are never fun, nor do they provoke laughter and frolicking. However, if we allow our mindsets to turn negative and focus on only the bad things, then we will be easily defeated. However, focusing on the positive of every situation—the aspects of that situation that will strengthen and progress you—will allow you to find your way out of the darkness into the glorious light.

Patience endures the darkness while focusing your attention on the small glimmer of light. It doesn't mean that you don't feel anger, frustration, fear, or pain. It means that you don't allow these feelings to control your behavior. When struggling, patience tells you to "stand still and see the salvation of the Lord" (Exod.14:13). Moses had to display patience when he reached the Red Sea and Pharaoh's army was behind. The patience he exercised in what seemed like a dead end allowed him to focus on the one glimmer of light he had—the ability to seek God's counsel.

When he stopped and asked for instruction, God spoke and said,

> "Wherefore criest thou unto me? speak unto the children of Israel, that they go forward: But lift thou up thy rod, and stretch out thine hand over the sea, and divide it: and the children of Israel shall go on dry ground through the midst of the sea" (Exod. 14:16).

Isn't that often how God works? While we are complaining, God is waiting for us to come to Him so that He can give us the instruction we need.

Much can be written about patience, but there is one last aspect of patience that we must understand as maturing Christians. For emphasis, I'll say it like this—SHUT UP! Lamentations 3:26 put it best: "It is good that a man should both hope and *quietly* wait for the salvation of the Lord." Why did the author have to use the word "quietly"? It's simple; many times we cause more damage with the words we say than the fate that awaited us. God has established immutable laws of nature. You are familiar with some of these laws, such as "what goes up, must come down;"—the law of gravity.

Likewise, one of these laws is found in Proverbs 18:21: "Life and death are in the power of the tongue." We delay and sometimes even destroy the blessings stored up for us because of what we say during a time of stress or frustration. The children of Israel were held back from the Promised Land for 40 years because in their impatience they began to murmur and complain. Patience is best accompanied by silence. As our teachers and mothers told us: "If you don't have anything good to say, don't say anything at all." It may be those words of doubt or negativity that cause you to lose your victory.

CHAPTER 9

FORGIVENESS

Finally, we will end this section the same way Jesus ended His earthly life 2000 years ago—with forgiveness. If anyone had a reason to hold a grudge, it was Jesus. If anyone had reason to go to the Judge and demand retribution, it was Jesus! Jesus came to the world having done no sin, but was punished with the worst of criminals. Jesus "went to His own, and His own received Him not," but instead arranged for His execution. Yet, after all of this, Jesus' last words were "Father forgive them, for they know not what they do" (Luke 23:34).

Can you do that? Can you endure the rejection and sabotage of others and have a heart that desires only the well being and forgiveness of your enemies? Well, if you want to become a mature Christian, this will be one of your tests. The question is not "what will you do if it happens?" The question is "what will you do *when* it happens?"

Forgiveness is like the final exam of Christian maturity. It was the final request of Jesus before His death on the Cross, and God honored that request by touching the heart of the thief on the cross beside Jesus to ask "remember me when thou comest into thy kingdom." Here, God responded to Jesus request through this thief's request, letting Jesus know that the forgiveness had been granted and that all men may come in humility to Jesus for forgiveness and eternal life.

Are you ready to mature? Are you ready to address your unforgiving heart? Yes, I believe that you have forgiven a lot of people, but if you have one person that you have not forgiven, then you still have an unforgiving heart. One of the most touted statements when it comes to forgiveness is: "I can forgive, but I don't have to forget." That is a sign that you have not forgiven. I don't debate the validity of learning from the past in order to prevent future problems. If you have a friend or relative who is prone to steal from you, you should not allow that person to hold your purse in the name of forgiveness. However, if you say you love and forgive that person, you embrace them and tell them, "I forgive you for stealing from me. I forgive the debt as well. Whatever you took from me is gone and I don't require it back. I will continue to desire the best for you and help you in anyway that I can within reason. "

After you have forgiven that person, you must take the next step and do as God did—"throw it into the depths of the sea" (Mic 7:19.) In other words, don't bring it up again. Don't use that past deed as leverage to manipulate and attack that person in the future. When you truly forgive, you may have recollection of an offense but that offense no longer takes authority in your emotional response to the offender. When you see that person, you no longer get that gut-wrenching de-sire to give that person a piece of your mind. You no longer feel uncomfortable in their presence or hope for them to feel uncomfortable in yours.

Can you imagine if you went to heaven and the first thing Jesus did was walk up to you and say in an accusatory tone, "Hey, look at these scars, this is all because you wouldn't stop lying. I had to go through all of this and it's all your fault. I would show you around the Kingdom, but my feet hurt too badly from these nail holes, thanks to you!"

Instead, Jesus waits with open arms for our return. He longs for it. And when we get there, He will wrap His arms around us like the father of the prodigal son. He will drape us in His loving embrace with all of the acceptance and love He has to offer. There will be no mention of our past wrongs, no mention of what He had to go through to get you back, only an abiding love.

The question you must ask yourself is this: If Jesus could forgive, who was 100% God, but was spit upon, degraded, in-sulted, and killed, who am I that I don't have to forgive? In fact, if Jesus was REQUIRED by God to forgive then who are we that we don't have to forgive?

Development

CHAPTER 10

Development

What was Jesus doing from age 12 to 30? We all know His conception story, His Birth story, and then His attempt to run away from home and go full-time in the ministry at the ripe old age of 12 (I speak lightheartedly of course). What happened in between? I submit to you that for 18 years Jesus was developing his mind and body for His three year mission. Although we don't hear about Jesus' life between these ages, we do find out in Luke 4:16 that it was Jesus' "custom" to go to the synagogue on the Sabbath. Therefore we realize that although He was God wrapped in flesh, Jesus still studied the Word and listened to others preach the Word while on earth. Therefore, just as the Son of God had to develop, so must we develop in our Christian walks. In this section of the book, I will discuss a number of areas where Christians must develop.

Developing in Christ can't be done overnight. The disciples were taught for three and a half years and still did not fully comprehend the magnitude of the Savior until the supernatural move of the Holy Ghost brought full enlightenment. As a matter of the fact, the majority of them did not believe

that He was the Son of God until after His death and resurrec-
tion.

So, as you are struggling to be the mature Christian you
desire to be, contrary to the thoughts of yesteryear, it does not
mean that you are not moving in the right direction. Years ago,
we were taught that if you were struggling to live right, it was
because you were not truly saved. As a matter of fact, they said
you didn't have the Holy Ghost if you had to struggle to live
right.

As I matured in Christ, I came to understand the shear
hypocrisy of this notion. I believe this black-or-white interpretation of holiness forces, to a certain extent, the hypocrisy we
find so rampant in the Church. I am not promulgating a
"permissive" theology that accepts sin, but I do believe that as
long as you are making progressive steps to overcome sin, then
you are heading in the right direction. Instead, we have forced
people to lie to themselves and to the Body in order to maintain a false image of righteousness. This impedes our development, for while we should be getting help in overcoming our
issues, we cannot receive that help because we are condemned
for having the issues in the first place.

Many of us know people in the Church who said they
never did any wrong and we try to identify with them and say
the same thing. We claim to have done no wrong since coming
to Christ. As a result, we are conflicted in our faith, and constantly walking in a state of guilt. We don't truly enjoy the
grace and mercy provided by the Cross. This is not to say that

you should go out and do wrong. As Paul said, "What then? Shall we sin, because we are not under the law, but under grace? God forbid" (Rom.6:15). This grace and mercy provides us with an Advocate with the Father through Jesus Christ. Because of Jesus, we can go before God and ask for forgiveness. One of the greatest tools you have toward your Christian maturity or development thereof is the tool of repentance.

There is nothing wrong with saying to God, "Lord forgive me." You may have a problem if you come to the Church and tell all the wrong you have done because sometimes people won't forgive you but God will always forgive you. God will forget about those things that you have done when people won't.

Everybody makes mistakes. I've made some since I've been preaching as a pastor. I will not be put on a pedestal and be made an idol to anyone. I'm not going to pretend to have attained perfection. The fact that I'm still walking around on this earth should be a sign that I have not reached the point of perfection because if I were perfect, I would be in heaven. I know it's strange for a pastor—and even more a Bishop—to make such a declaration because most people seek applause. I don't seek applause because I know I can't live off of it. I can't take it to the bank and it won't help me sleep at night. Only the truth will help me develop.

CHAPTER 11

Develop in Purpose: Know Your Calling

It is important that we understand Christian Maturity in relationship to service. Service to the Body of Christ can only be done through the Spirit. Cleaning the church parking lot is not a spiritual act, but the spirit in which you clean the parking lot is. God has given each and every person a spiritual gift to empower us to serve the Kingdom. Mature Christians must understand and utilize their spiritual gift to fulfill their calling in the Body.

We know that the Holy Ghost gives to us different gifts. In 1 Cor. 12:11 we learn, "But all these worketh that one and the selfsame Spirit, dividing to every man severally as he will." Whatever gift God has given to you, you should know it for yourself. You should never have to go to anybody and ask them, "what is the gift I have working for me? What is my calling?" You should know what your calling is.

Even as we look at the vision of the Church and as we have departmentalized our vision, you need to know in what area you should work. How do you know that? Let me give you one simple clue. Is there anything you like to do better than anything else in the Church? Is there anything you feel more comfortable in doing than anything else in the Church? It's what you enjoy doing.

God did not call you into what you don't enjoy doing. Paul was a tremendous orator, teacher, trainer, a gatherer of people and so when Jesus called him, He called him into that of an Apostle. Jesus didn't tell Paul to become a choir director, or an usher. He didn't call Paul to lead the building fund campaigns. He utilized Paul's strengths as an effective communicator and influential citizen. He allowed Paul to take all of that knowledge he had and use it for the Kingdom. Get out there and preach and teach and show the people. There are things you can do in the Church. Know what your gifts are and then work in your gifts.

Balance Your Gift

Read through the entire 12th Chapter of 1 Corinthians and understand it. Once you find out what your spiritual gifts are, be faithful in using the gifts. With your gift comes great responsibility, and we must be balanced to use it correctly. Don't use your gifts like the bellboy syndrome. Don't ring your spiritual bell whenever you need Jesus to work for you or whenever you want to impress a group. Use your gifts all of the time as the Lord instructs you. The Church needs your gifts.

Also, don't use your gifts for damnation. If you have the gift of prophecy, don't walk up to people saying, "Thus saith the Lord, thou shalt surely die. All those of you who wear red dresses; those who eat too much shall go to hell." God does not send those kinds of messages. That may seem far fetched, but some of the prophecies I have heard in the Church are just as bad. God gives gifts to help bring us together; to set us on fire; to build us up; to make us strong; to fortify us, give us strength so that we can go through the trials of life.

Of course, don't be timid about using your gifts. If God gives you a message of rebuke, it is imperative that you warn the people. God told Ezekiel,

> "When I say unto the wicked, Thou shalt surely
> die; and thou givest him not warning, nor speak-
> est to warn the wicked from his wicked way, to
> save his life; the same wicked [man] shall die in
> his iniquity; but his blood will I require at thine
> hand" (Ezekiel 3:18).

You don't always have to be seen to use your gifts. If God tells you to pray for someone, go meet that person privately and simply tell them, "the Lord told me to pray with you." Anybody will receive prayer. You don't have to stand up in the middle of an event or church service and tell everyone you have a "word" for the sister in the third row. I remember once asking a minister to give the benediction for a service. I had already preached what God gave me to preach and the Spirit had already moved in the service. This minister got up and began to call out a woman in the crowd with a "word."

I immediately informed him that his responsibility was to give the benediction only. If the Spirit had given him a word for that young lady, the Spirit would have had him move at the appropriate time. This minister was taking the opportunity to appear "spiritually deep," only to show how truly shallow he was. The Bible tells us the "spirits of the prophets are subject to the prophets, for God is not the author of confusion" (1 Corinthians 14:32-33). God is not going to give the pastor of a church a Word and then bring another person onto the pulpit to deliver a different word. When we mature in Christ, we don't have to be seen in our service to God. We know that what we do in private will be rewarded by God in the open.

You don't have to have an audience. Don't approach your pastor and ask to hold a two week revival because the Lord has anointed you to heal people. If He has anointed you to heal people then start healing them. You don't have to have a revival to heal. Just go on and start healing and call those who need to be healed. You don't have to call all of us, we may not all need healing. Just get those who need to be healed.

When I was taught this, I took it at face value. When I first was anointed with the gift of healing, I went straight to the hospital. I walked on every floor; I went into every room. I will never forget one lady was in a traction splint. A traction splint is commonly used to treat complete long bone fractures of the leg, femur or tibia and fibula area. She had the brace on and I walked up to her and laid my hands upon her and said, "in the name of Jesus, get up and walk."

She evidently felt God's healing power because she didn't laugh and tell me to get out of her room. Instead she asked the nurse to take the splint off. The nurse said she could not do that until the doctor approved. I told her to call him. I was 17 years old and the gifts were working.

The doctor came and wanted to know who this young boy was who was taking his patients away. I told him I was a servant of the Lord and that I had the anointing of God and that woman was healed. The doctor asked her if she still had the pain, and she told him she did not. I told him to examine her and see. He examined her and she did not show any signs of experiencing pain. The doctor ordered the nurse to remove the splint. He was just as eager to see this miracle as anyone else. The nurse removed the splint and she walked right out of that hospital that day.

After that, I went to rooms where patients had tumors and laid my hands upon them, told them to be healed in the name of Jesus, and they were healed. I believed what the Word of God said, God had given me a gift and I did not let anything keep me from exercising it. I went to the hospital and prayed for the people; I went to the nursing homes and prayed for the people; I went to the rest homes and prayed for the people; I didn't try to seek some kind of revival. I just wanted to use my spiritual gift.

There are plenty of sick people to be healed; plenty of distressed people who could use prayer, plenty of broken hearted people who could use a word of encouragement, and most importantly, these people are not all found in the four walls of your local church. We often only want to use our gifts amongst each other. We have totally missed the point. Jesus did not do miracles for the church. He performed miracles for the lost. We must not confuse the statement "Use your gifts for the Church" to mean that we only use our gift *in* the Church. We use our gifts to build the Church. That means going outside of the church to bring people into the church.

Does God still use people today? He sure does. Be faithful in using your gifts and be Spirit empowered. Don't be weak, be vibrant. Have the empowerment of the Spirit.

CHAPTER 12

Develop In Esteem: Know Who You Are

When you are Christlike, you know who you are in Him. Just as Jesus knew who He was in the eyes of the Father, we should know who we are in Christ. Romans 8:1 states, "There is therefore now no condemnation to them which are in Christ Jesus, who walk not after the flesh, but after the Spirit." When you accept who you are, you know that in Christ Jesus there is no condemnation, but outside of Him there is. In other words, what makes you who you are is the fact that you are in Him. Without the shedding of His blood; without the fact that He has given to us redemption, we are lost.

There is nothing about us that has changed other than our faith. We are yet born in sin, we yet sin, and we are yet unworthy of the grace and mercy of God. When we submit to the Lordship of Jesus Christ, He covers us [hides and shields us] with His blood. That means that He brings us in as we are, and exempts us from the just punishment that we deserve for being who we are. This is the reason the Scripture says, "the just shall live by faith" (Heb. 10:38). Our faith makes us who we are in Him.

Accepting who you are means you understand that you are no better and no worse than your neighbor. We often times make the mistake of equating who we are with the material goods we have. We call a person with affluence, "blessed." We consider this person to have it all together. We feel he or she is somehow better than we are. We confuse this somehow with a proper standing with God.

However, Jesus asked the question, "For what shall it profit a man, if he shall gain the whole world, and lose his own soul?"(Mark 8:36). Great wealth never equates to great relationships; be it natural or spiritual. Who we are can only be found in our relationship with God. You need to accept who you are in Him. Don't go back to thinking on how terrible you have been; know who you are now. You are risen with Christ; "you are a new creature, old things are passed away, and behold all things are become new" (2 Cor. 5:17).

This, however, does not mean for us to turn a blind eye to our sinful natures. We must know and come to grips with our weakness. It is a fatal mistake to ignore your weakness. Many people turn away from the ugly side of life, hoping that if they starve it of attention it will simply go away. Not so. In fact, quite the opposite happens. The enemy wants you to ignore it, because ignoring it leaves the door wide open for him to come and go as he pleases.

You don't focus on your weakness as a means to put yourself down. You don't focus on your weaknesses as some pious exercise of humility. You definitely don't focus on your weakness as a way to excuse yourself for inappropriate behavior. You recognize your weakness in the sense that you rely on God's grace and anointing to keep you daily. You recognize your weakness in the sense that you don't look down your nose at others but help your brothers who are caught in sin, knowing that you too could be in the same situation.

Knowing your strengths is equally important. Having a balanced knowledge of your limitations and strengths will also keep you from becoming overly confident. I make it a point not to allow anyone to make me feel that I am more than I am. Some people will pat you on your back and flatter you with words that they don't mean. In fact, the Bible tells us that a "flattering tongue worketh ruin" (Prov. 26:28). The mature Christian must know when those flattering words don't meet up to God's measurements of him or her.

When people come up to me and tell me, "Pastor you sure can preach!" I can confidently and rightfully tell them, "I know I can." I know I can preach, not because I'm a great orator; I know I can preach because God has anointed me to preach. I know this is my strength because it is God who strengthened me to do what I am doing. If I get up and only say two words that the Lord has told me to say, then I have

CHRISTIAN MATURITY   87

preached a great sermon. If someone comes to me and says, "Bishop, you are the best preacher in the world. Nobody has a message like yours." I give that statement no consideration and know not to trust another word coming out of that person's mouth.

First of all, they have not heard every preacher in the world. Secondly, my messages come from God. So I can never take claim of a unique message when I am not the originator of that message. Likewise, you should be bold and confident enough to proclaim the strengths that God has given you. If it did not come from God, have no confidence in it because it can be taken from you in the blinking of an eye. However, "the gifts and calling of God are without repentance" (Rom. 11:29). Don't ever let your ego be inflated because the same people who inflate your ego will stick a pin in it and bring you down.

We Are Not the Same

Mature Christians also know they are not islands unto themselves. Paul exhorts us in Romans 12:3 "not to think [of himself] more highly than he ought to think; but to think soberly, according as God hath dealt to every man the measure of faith." We cannot get so caught up into our own visions and ministries that we believe everyone should be involved in that which we are involved.

Some preachers believe they are the only people who can deliver the Word of God. We must realize there is always someone who can take God's message and teach it much better. God does not stop with one person. That's the reason He called twelve disciples and not one. And they were not all alike. As Paul explains in verses 4-6 "For as we have many members in one body, and all members have not the same office: So we, [being] many, are one body in Christ, and every one members one of another."

God saved all of us and we are not all alike. We have different degrees of intelligence. Some are smarter than others; some study more than others; some are gifted and some are not. Whatever it may be, all of us make one and together we make a force. Together, we make a powerful Church; together, we make an anointed Church.

CHAPTER 13

Develop in Giving

As Christians, we need to know how to develop in giving to others. When you are involved in Christian maturity you are unselfish with others. You are willing to share. The Scripture explains the concept of giving like this: "Give and it shall be given unto you, good measure, pressed down, shaken together and running over shall men give unto your bosom" (Luke 6:38).

We must give because God gives. John 3:16 shows us that God loved us so that He "gave." All of the silver, all of the gold, all of our possessions collectively in this whole entire universe will not equal the Gift that God has given to mankind, in the person of Jesus the Christ. If we are in Him, we must have the same posture that He has; He is a God that's unselfish.

When you mature, you learn to give to each other. One Saturday, my church blessed me financially with $2,000. They gave me the envelope with the money and I immediately asked God, "Lord, what do you want me to do with these funds?" I wanted to put the money back into the church building fund but the Lord informed me there were four families that needed the money. Two of the families were in Nashville and two in another city. I gave up that money because God told me to. I could have kept it! I could have used it, but I would have been out of the will of God. As we mature in the Lord, we have to be unselfish and willing to share what we have. I had a child who could have used that money, but God didn't tell me to give it to my child.

When you give, you must give as God gives direction. I was not going to run out in the streets and find the first person who needed something. Even your good intentions, if done outside of the complete will of God can get you into a mess of trouble. You have to do as God ordains. When you obey God in sharing, God has somebody out there who has more than you have, who is going to give unto you. Satan, on the other hand, will magnify what you have received and try to convince you to use it for your own gain. He will try to convince you that God is not speaking to you.

Christian maturity lets you know when to share and how to be unselfish. You may be wondering why I would say "when to share." Believe it or not, there is a time when we should give and when we should not give. The fact is, sometimes God will not want you to give someone a handout. Sometimes that person needs wisdom. We've all heard the saying "give a man a fish and he will eat for a day; teach him to fish and he will eat for a lifetime." Sometimes people are abusers of the givers. God is not going to allow you to be abused.

It is imperative that we hear God's voice as it relates to our giving. Even in the church setting, I teach my congregation to seek God's voice on what they should give in an offering. I teach them not to be moved by preachers who promise a new car in the driveway if they give $100 in a special offering. If God does not tell you to give the $100, then do not expect a new car. Only through obedience to God will you find the riches of life.

When you pay tithe, that 10 percent is not yours. You are giving God what's His. So then, the real area of flexibility is in offering. Some folks will only give $1.00 in the offering. Yet they wonder why their finances are not blessed. In reality, God has blessed their gift. God has blessed them with another dollar for the dollar they gave. If they would only realize that God could bless them with more if they gave more. If you sow one seed in the ground, you will only reap from that one seed. If you sow many seeds, you will reap many times more.

Many times, you will find that the very thing that you want is what God will tell you to give up. If you give it up, believe me, the blessing is right around the corner for you, but you have to mature and develop in your giving.

Giving Your Strength

There is another aspect of giving that we often overlook. When we hear the word "give" we immediately gravitate to money, but we must also consider giving of your spiritual strength. In relationships with others, we bear others' burdens. The word of God says, the strong ought to bear the infirmities of the weak (Rom. 15:1).

The Word states, "There is one body, and one Spirit, even as ye are called in one hope of your calling" (Eph. 4:4). If we are one body, we must bear one another's burdens. If your right leg is weak, your left leg gets stronger to carry you. If you lose vision in the right eye, the left eye gains a keener sight. If you lose strength in the right hand, the left hand gets stronger. The purpose is to help the body. Similarly, as one person within the Church gets weak, the rest of us must become strong so that we can carry that person until that person can carry himself or herself.

As we mature, we must learn to share our strengths to empower the Body. We are not walking in a boastful manner that shines a spotlight on ourselves. Instead we are empowering others with our strength. Unto everyone of us is given grace according to the measure of the gift of Christ. Christ gives us a special amount of strength. If I can handle grace and its abundance greater than you can, He is going to give me suffering so that I can help you through your time. That's the reason some mature with greater rapidity than others in the Church.

This is an aspect of Christian maturity that many people do not want to face. We do not want to believe that we are forced to go through hardships for no other reason than to be of assistance to another person. If many of us could have it our way, we would "live and let live." Our mentality would be, "I'll handle my problems, and you handle yours." However, that's not God's way.

I get excited when I think about the fact that I can help. It's a great thing to help somebody in the Church through a trying period in life—to be able to tell them that I've gone through the same trouble and let them know that they can get through it, too. When you see somebody who is not making it spiritually, you should use all of the energy that God has given you to carry them through.

Let's take Jesus for example. Jesus could have remained on His heavenly throne and said, "Father, let's start all over. In fact, don't save Noah or his family, let's just start anew." Instead, Jesus left heaven and used every ounce of His strength and energy to preach to this wicked world. He ministered for hours upon hours. Then He submitted to being brutally murdered. After which, Jesus was given all power in heaven and earth.

What did He do with that new level of power? He didn't go up to heaven to sit on a throne. Instead, He redirected that energy to go down into Hell to free those who died before He went to the cross. He took the keys to the gates of Hell and conquered death and the grave. Then, He ascended back to His Father. He didn't stop there. Now, He utilizes His considerable influence to be an advocate—a defense attorney—before the eternal Judge. He is not there poised with His royalty; He is not there with rubies and diamonds, and a crown on His head. Rather, He is there ensuring that we receive mercy. He is using His strength to bring us through this trial we call life. He uses all of His strengths to protect us in our weakness.

He is bearing our burdens; saying to God, "Lord have mercy. Don't destroy them, let them turn another leaf, give them another opportunity. They will make it God. I died for them, and You promised me that I would lose none that You have given to me." Jesus gave himself for us. As He bore our grief, let us bear one another's burdens. As we mature, we will reach out and help.

CHAPTER 14

Develop in Wholesome Thought

As we deal with Christian Maturity in Christ likeness, one of the real problems that we have is that we don't have wholesome thoughts and we need to have a wholesome "thought life" in order to experience Christian maturity. Too many people think negatively. Our nation is consumed with the negatives of life; the drama. One of the reasons we think so much about bad things is that we are so busy watching television.

Every time you turn on the television there is something negative; somebody got killed, economy is going down, wars and terrorist attacks. In the midst of this, Philippians 4:8 encourages us,

> "FINALLY, brethren, whatsoever things are true, whatsoever things are honest, whatsoever things are just, whatsoever things are pure,

whatsoever things are lovely, whatsoever things
are of good report; if there be any virtue, and if
there be any praise, think on these things."

This passage of scripture is not saying you will never
have impure thoughts, or thoughts of injustice, or thoughts of
untruth. This passage is showing us how to control our
thoughts. Whenever we experience unlovely thoughts, which
we will, this passage instructs us to think on "whatsoever
things are lovely." To experience true growth, let's delve into
how we can apply wholesome thought life.

Things That Are True

Who are you? What are you about? What is your relationship with God? How do you stand with Him? How do you
relate to each other? Think on those things that are true. Don't
think in terms of fantasy. It is okay to have dreams to which
you aspire, but the operative word is "aspire". That means you
are working towards this goal, slowly and methodically. You
don't live a life of pretense. You are truthful with yourself and
you walk in truth.

This is one of the fundamentals of Christian maturity.
So many Christians are not maturing because they are unable
to face the truth about who they *truly* are, what they are *truly*

about, what their *true* relationship with God is about, and how they *truly* relate with others.

As a result, these people live a life of pretense which blinds them. This mask they wear blocks their vision, keeping them from seeing the path to true growth. These people are so focused on the way they want things to be, they choose not to deal with how things really are. A prime example of not dealing with truth can be found in the recent foreclosure epidemic our nation experienced. So many people ignored their true financial standing. They opted, instead, to obtain "creative" loans in order to live a dream. Unfortunately, we must all wake up from dreams, and the national mortgage was the real-life nightmare to which many of us opened our eyes.

On a spiritual parallel, many of us are doing the same thing when it comes to our spiritual homes. Instead of seeking the truth in the Word of God, we, as the Bible says in 2 Timothy 4:3, "will not endure sound doctrine; but after their own lusts shall they heap to themselves teachers, having itching ears." We are becoming a Church that only wants to hear the good tidings of riches and forgiveness. We feed on the sweets of the Gospel and forsake the vegetables. Just like the balloon mortgages, this floating balloon will soon reach its popping point.

We pay homage to the pastors of the "mega churches" and allow them to spoon feed us any doctrine they choose because they have a large following. We don't weigh their charisma against the Word of God. Time after time we have witnessed "superstar" preachers make great spectacles of themselves and the Christian faith. As a result, many souls are damaged and offended.

However, in the face of these ministers' indiscretions, we are also provided the opportunity to extend another application of walking in the truth. When you think on the truth, you can honestly consider your own inabilities and mistakes; your own failures. When you do that, it helps you to understand others. No person is exempt from doing or saying something that removes him or her from the will of God. In fact, we are all only one decision from being in the same position as the person at whom we look down our noses.

When we consider those things that are true, we are not so quick to judge and condemn. I recall a situation with my daughter, Misha, who had done something I did not want her to do. She was on her way up the stairs and I told her to come back down. I had taken off my belt and was getting ready to give her a spanking when the Lord spoke to me and said, "Jerry, won't you treat her the way I treat you when you mess up?"

I put my belt back in my pants and told her to go upstairs. The truth of the matter is, there are times when I have disobeyed God and He had mercy on me. Instead of punishing me, He allowed me to grow up and mature. He covered me in His love and sheltered me from His wrath. Many times, that grace and mercy can do more to straighten you out than punishment. Some of us make large mistakes in our lives, others small mistakes, but a mistake is a mistake.

We must weigh all things to the truth. Truth is not emotional. Truth is not always soothing and comforting. However, truth is always freeing. As John 8:32 tells us, "ye shall know the truth, and the truth shall make you free."

Whatsoever Things Are Honest

Honesty, according to the Holman Bible dictionary, is defined as "fairness and straightforwardness of conduct." In the Bible, honesty is also synonymous with acting honorable or with dignity. In chapter one, we discussed those who lie and wait to deceive. Do you have a scheming mind? Do you think of ways to cut corners or find loopholes? Many people become "honesty-challenged" around the same time of the year—tax season. I use this example because it is very easy to point the finger at the corner hustler or the con artist, but we see ourselves through rose-colored glasses.

In actuality, when you create fake expenses for a tax write off; when you claim your neighbors or other family members' children on your taxes; or—even more common—when you pay someone $50 so that they can go purchase you $100 worth of groceries with their food stamps, then you are no more honest, honorable, and have no more dignity than the armed robber or shoplifter. Yes, God does have a strict standard for the mature Christians to do ALL things with honesty. We are to think only upon the honest and honorable approach.

Honesty sometimes seems to put you at the bottom of the pack. We've all heard the old saying, "nice guys finish last." That's how being honest makes you feel at times. However, we cannot grow in Christ until we can be honest in all things. Many have heard televangelist Joyce Meyer discuss how God took her through a season of what "seemed like the most strict and petty training in honest living." She talks about how God would convict her to "put the grocery cart back in the cart rack [instead of leaving it in the parking lot]." She talked about how she dropped a small piece of paper –barely recognizable--on the floor accidentally and kept walking but God made her turn around and walk all the way back to pick up that paper.

It is this level of pure honest and honorable living that God requires of His people. Some people truly do not believe God requires that level of discipline from His people. They fail to grasp the fundamental strength within such principles. Big things are composed of little things. In fact, everything you see is made up of microscopic particles called atoms. You'll never see an atom with the naked eye, but without these invisible molecular organisms, nothing would exist.

Likewise, your honesty, honor, integrity and dignity may never be seen, but without it, your full purpose will never be realized. You have to master the small things in order to be trusted with the big things. As Jesus explained in His parable, if you will be "faithful over a few things," He will make you "ruler over many things." If you are prone to seek shortcuts, cut corners or flat out lie, steal, and cheat to get what you want, then God cannot use you.

When you struggle to walk in honesty, you are really struggling to trust God. Why do we lie, steal, or cheat? We do so out of fear that circumstances will not work out in our favor if we do not intervene. Usually, however, our lying and cheating makes things worse than if we had just walked in honesty. When we lie, we have to keep lying in order to cover the last lie. When we steal, we can't enjoy that which we have stolen because we don't want others to know we have it. The cycle is brutal. When we trust in God completely, we know we don't have to intervene because "we know that all things work together for good to them that love God, to them who are the called according to [his] purpose" (Rom. 8:28). If you can't trust God to keep you, then you are not ready to be used by God.

Whatsoever Things Are Just

Are you a just person? Justice is a critical component of Christian maturity because God is just. Justice and being "just" dictates the quality of man's relationship one to another. Justice serves two primary objectives. First, which is most common, to provide legal balance—ensuring penalties are meted out to those who break laws, as well as protecting victims who have been treated unjustly. Secondly, more unrecognized, Justice provides equal opportunity for all men to enjoy the advantages of life, as noted in Deuteronomy 10:17-18:

> "For the LORD your God is the God of gods and the Lord of lords, the great, the mighty, and the awesome God who does not show partiality nor take a bribe. He executes justice for the orphan and the widow, and shows His love for the alien by giving him food and clothing" (NASB).

More than not, the Bible references justice to shed light on man's treatment to man. God wants us to have a "just" mindset. A mindset that seeks the benefit of all of mankind—especially the poor, orphaned, elderly, and widowed. What is just? Is it providing the basic necessities of life to only those who fit within your scope of comfort or only to those whom you admire? No, it is as the previous scripture tells us. Justice means showing "no partiality", "taking no bribes" but showing every man, woman, and child the highest level of your consideration and concern.

During this year of election and political strife, we have seen the ultimate test of this concept of justice. We have seen the fiercest opposition to the ideal of providing healthcare to all American citizens. People are threatening to kill politicians who have voted for this legislation. Let's truly consider what we are seeing. We live in the richest country on the face of the earth, where we pay individuals more than $60 million to play a game of football or basketball, where Corporate CEOs receive pat-on-the-back bonus checks totaling in the BILLIONS of dollars, yet we have become enraged at the idea of extending health insurance to those who cannot afford it.

Am I contesting the income levels of the aforementioned? Not at all. America enjoys a capitalist system, which has its pros and cons. One of the pros is that any person from any background can come to this country and utilize his or her mind, skills, and talents to amass a fortune for him or herself. The con is that many times this system breeds exploitation and abuse. We are watching now as Wall Street Bankers are being exposed for exploiting the market, gambling with people's hard -earned money and leaving them with the bad debt.

While we may embrace the opportunities this cultural system affords us, we must also balance our great freedoms with the Word of God. We cannot allow our wealth to callous our hearts to the needy. Are we displaying a just mind when we are willing to pay $10 for a bag of popcorn at a football game, but are willing to kill politicians who raise our taxes $1.00 to provide for a social service? As we grow in the Body, we must take on the just mindset of Christ. This mindset shows no partiality, but provides love for all men, whether they be of high or low esteem.

Whatsoever Things Are Pure

When you grow in Christian Maturity, your conversations and your thoughts change. You no longer see with the eyes of the world. How does the world see life? The world has become more and more lust-driven. When water commercials utilize sex as a means of promotion, we have lost our purity. Movies 30 years ago were rated PG-13 if there was a fist-fight seen. Now, cursing, mild nudity, and murder are considered appropriate for preteens.

We are living in a world that believes the raunchier, more violent, and more sexual, the better. We as Christians stand in the midst of a modern day Sodom and Gomorrah, just as Lot and his family once faced. We must refrain from absorbing the environment and be a light in this darkness. By thinking on those things which are pure, we continuously keep our thought patterns in check with the will of God.

What is purity? Of course, the first thing we think of is sexuality. This is common because our country now runs on it. However, the true definition of purity is a "state of being or process of becoming free of inferior elements or ritual uncleanness. What are inferior elements to the mature Christian? Anything that does not line up with the will and Word of God is an impurity. Whether it be small or large, "all unrighteousness is sin."

We must always direct our thoughts toward godly purity. When you wake up in the morning and just don't feel like going to work, ask yourself what the "pure" thing to do would be. Would it be to tell a "little white lie" to get out of work, or would it be to honor your agreement to work an honest day's work for an honest day's pay. When you are cut off on the interstate, consider the pure approach to dealing with the situation. Do you want to allow the dirty particles of cursing and waving that one finger to contaminate your spirit? Think on whatsoever is pure.

Whatsoever Things Are Lovely

We live in what is quickly becoming an ugly world. War, crime, terrorism, failed economy—the list goes on. If we focus all of our attention on the ugliness of this world, we will miss the beauty that God has placed before our eyes. In spite of the sin and corruption, God still wants us to enjoy a beautiful, lovely life. Beauty is in your mind's eye. That's why we must think on the lovely things God has given us.

Those who think everything will be ugly and terrible, will inevitably make everything ugly and terrible. The Bible tells us that "as he thinketh in his heart; so is he..." (Prov. 23:7). Mature Christians have the power to speak life and death into the environment, and we speak what we think, as we are told in Matthew 12:34 "Out of the abundance of the heart, the mouth speaketh." God would not have such powerful weapons used to bring about death. Therefore, it is imperative that we mature in speaking that which is lovely, in order to display and bring into fruition that which is "lovely."

Whatsoever Things Are of a Good Report

Listen to good reports. One of the highly effective habits of the world's most successful people is that they are always listening to self-help, developmental tapes, or reading books that concentrate on their specific area of expertise. They feed on this information because it strengthens their resolve, teaches them new information and makes them better at what they do. Successful people watch three times less television than the average person and rarely, if ever, listen to music radio.

In order to grow and become mature Christians, it is important that we think on good reports of the faith. The Word tells us "Faith comes by hearing." Good reports build our faith. By listening to the witness of fellow saints who have gone through tough times and come out, we have more strength to go through our own struggles. When we listen to people who come to us with junk, we are weakened.

When you meet negative people you should stop them right in their track or just turn and walk away. Challenge yourself to only listen to good reports. You don't have to listen to negativity. It is a choice. You also must not be the carrier of bad reports. If you learn something about a fellow Christian, keep it to yourself. Only talk to God about it. That's called prayer. Since your gossip partner can't change anyone's behavior, take your news to the One who can change a person's behavior—God.

Yes God already knows what happened; but did you ever consider the reason God allowed you to see it was because He wanted you to pray for the person? Instead of trying to find out the dirt on others, learn a whole lot about Jesus and tell people about Him. If there be any praise, think on these things. If you find it difficult to decide what to think on, take Paul's advice, "Those things, which ye have both learned, and received, and heard, and seen in me, do: and the God of peace shall be with you" (Phil. 4:9).

Paul was a person who understood the walk. He said, the things that you have seen me do, I want you to do those things and I want you to think on those things. "Mark the perfect man and behold the upright" (Ps. 37:37). Jesus is that man. Have a good mind—a healthy mind. Have a healthy spirit. You cannot do that dealing with junk. People who eat junk food all of the time usually have a junky body. If you eat a lot of junk spiritually, you will have a junky life. If you want a wholesome thought life, then you have to deal with wholesome food and that's found in the Holy Writ.

CHAPTER 15

Develop in Kindness

When we think about the holiday season, Thanksgiving through New Years, there is something about that period of time that causes people to act differently. Have you ever noticed how some people hardly speak to you throughout the year but during this particular time they suddenly become very close and they want to talk to you more? Even your boss who has been on your case all year will start smiling. Unfortunately, these warm feelings only last until January 2.

Kindness is not to be something that you conjure up for the moment or that you introduce because of a season. Kindness must be a part of your character. Romans 12:10 states, "Be kindly affectioned one to another with brotherly love; in honour preferring one another." The word "kindness" comes from the greek word which means "serviceable, good, pleasant and gracious." I focus on the word serviceable first because when you say you are serviceable, you are willing to do for others, to expend energy for others. That mentality should not come just during Thanksgiving and Christmas time, rather it should become a part of your daily life.

"Be kindly affectioned one to another with brotherly love" (Rom. 12:10). Brotherly love is closely akin to godly love—agape love. Agape love is an unconditional, ever flowing love. The Book of Hebrews instructs us to "let brotherly love continue" (Heb 13:1).

As our world becomes more and more automated, and as we become more reliant upon technology and less upon our fellow man, it seems we are losing the neighborly kindness and affection that we used to have. Instead of driving past a person and waving, we now experience road rage. People are literally ready to fight and kill because the other driver is driving too slowly.

Unfortunately, this lack of affection is not just in the world; we also see it in the Church. We need to learn to be affectionate and kind within the body of Christ. We greeted each other with a hug and kiss when I was growing up. Life wasn't so hard, cold and cutting. We were nice and warm in the way we treated each other.

1 Corinthians 13:4 states "Charity suffereth long, and is kind..." Charity is the Bible's term for "Love," and therefore, love is kind. In this chapter, Paul named every religious and spiritual act that we associate with "deep" Christians. He discussed speaking in tongues, prophesying, understanding mysteries, having the gift of knowledge and having strong faith to remove mountains. He discussed giving away all of his goods

and even giving his body to be burned. Yet, in all of this, he explained that if he did not have love, he was "nothing." He wrote that without love, "It profiteth me nothing" (v. 3).

Herein we find the true purpose of why we must be kind. Kindness is an element of the compound we call love. Without kindness, you don't have love, and love is the ticket into the gates of heaven. You cannot be a mature Christian without love and you cannot have love without kindness. God has placed us on this earth, not as islands unto ourselves, but as a community. Our purpose is to uplift each other through affection and encouragement. It was never God's intention for man to fight with one another, bringing each other down.

Unfortunately, we live in a world today where you are considered strange when you are kind. Have you ever met a person who just seemed to be "too nice." They always exude a smile and always look for the best in people. If I am to be completely honest, sometimes those people will get on your nerves because you can't go to them to talk about another person. You can't complain about the boss with that person. Believe it or not, that person is the perfect example of love manifested.

Look at Ephesians 4:32, which states, "be kind one to another, tenderhearted, forgiving one another, even as God for Christ's sake hath forgiven you." Individuals who look for the best in others are following this scripture perfectly. Being tender-hearted and forgiving is proof of Christian maturity and growth. The lack of maturity causes you to be quick to fight.

When you don't mature, you respond to people in a very negative way, and it doesn't matter to you who you hurt.

If you are a person who is quick to tell your feelings no matter how it affects the people around you, then you are a person who still has a lot of growing to do. I am not suggesting that you should suppress your convictions and allow emotions to pressurize. Even Jesus let a few people "have it" when the time was prudent. We must always be conscious of how our words will affect our neighbors in the long run. When you mature in the Spirit of the Lord, you are concerned about how your neighbor will be affected by your words because you love that individual.

When you love someone, you treat them as you want to be treated because you see that person as yourself. When you come into the body of Christ, we are one. Jesus said He gave us the glory that God gave Him so that "they may be one, even as we are one" (John 17:22). How were God and Jesus one? They were one in Spirit and in the Word.

As mature Christians, when we are filled with the Word, we are one with our fellow mature Christians. In essence we are running on the same program—the Word of God. Imagine putting two copies of the same CD in a CD player and pressing play at the exact same time. What would you hear? Would you hear two different songs playing? No, you would hear one, synchronized sound because both CD's have been programmed with the same songs. Likewise, when we are filled with the Spirit and the Word of God, we see each other as though we are looking in a mirror.

Sure, we come in different shapes, colors and sizes, but in spirit, there is no difference. When I treat you in any way less than the Word of God and the Spirit of God directs, then I should feel an immediate sense of conviction. I should know immediately that I am out of sync with the program—and vice versa.

If I'm in you and you are in me, then how could I not be kind to you? I will not try to find something negative about you and try to harm you. I will not try to catch you off in some kind of trap or make life miserable for you, because if I do that to you, I'm doing it to myself.

Components of Kindness

Colossians 3:12 "Put on therefore, as the elect of God, holy beloved, bowels of mercies, kindness, humbleness of mind, meekness, longsuffering." Notice what's going on here. In order for you to be kind, you also have to be humble. You cannot be kind and not be humble; you cannot be kind and not be meek. You cannot be kind over an extended period of time without a degree of longsuffering. You have to have all of these components because some people, as you all say, get on your "last nerve."

If you think that you can go through life being kind only to those who are kind to you, you need to wake up because there are some people who are kind to you tonight but, won't speak to you tomorrow. And guess what, they may be in your Church. It is your responsibility to show kindness to those who treat you this way.

The Word instructs us to "put on therefore as the elect of God..." You have to do it, don't ask God to make you kind. He is not going to do it. You have to make a decision to be kind! He told you to put it on.

CHAPTER 16

Develop Unity in the Spirit

If I have not been clear up to this point, I will reemphasize one of the greatest necessities of Christian maturity— relationship! In 1 John 4:20 the question is asked: "how can you say you love God who you cannot see, but hate your brother who you see everyday?" It is very important that we get along with our neighbors outside of the church. It is critical that we learn to get along with each other.

This is not to say loving the unsaved is not paramount, for it is, but we must be careful that we don't spend too much time socializing with our worldly counterparts. Paul warns us that "evil communications corrupt good manners" (1 Cor. 15:33). Therefore, though we should love and have healthy relationship with those outside of the Body, our strength and survival in the faith depends on our ability to maintain mature, strong relationships within the Body.

We come to the house of the Lord and become a part of the body of Christ so that we can work together to affect change within the community, within our homes, and so that we may advance the Word of God. It is our responsibility to be exemplary in our behavior so that others may understand who this God is that we serve. When we exemplify strong, balanced relationships and an environment of love, concern, and nurture, this will cause the world to want to serve God as we do; to worship Him and to magnify Him.

As we mature, we must have unity of the Spirit. Paul admonished the Church of Ephesus to "endeavor to keep the unity of the Spirit in the bond of peace" (Eph. 4:3). We must learn to walk in the Spirit. Without the Spirit we don't have anything in common. When we have that unity in the spirit, we have the power to win the lost. We can not win the world by ourselves. It was the Spirit of Jesus, not His body, that caused demons to flee and sickness to be healed.

The Sons of Sceva had to learn this truth the hard way. They thought they could speak the same jargon, act the same way, and get the same results. They figured they could use the name of Jesus and Paul as a reference and get respect. The Bible tells us that the demon told them "Jesus I know, and Paul I know, but who are you?" (Acts 19:15). In other words, the evil spirits don't respond to, nor are they bound by, any fleshly acts of religiosity. They are only subject to a unified spirit with God.

Let's take a true look at the significance of the demon's response. This demon did not say "Jesus, I have heard of"; the demon said "Jesus, I Know." The word "know" in the greek is *gnosis,* which is defined as a "spiritual knowledge." This demon explained to the sons of sceva that it had a "spiritual knowledge" of who Paul was and who Jesus was. This was not from mere acquaintance. The demon, more than likely, had never had a run in with Jesus or Paul, otherwise it would have been cast out. It knew exactly who they were because Jesus and Paul operated by the same Spirit.

Likewise, the world knows when the Church is not walking in a spirit of unity. The reason the Church has lost its influence in our communities today is because the world does not have a "gnosis" of the Body—a spiritual knowledge. The more Christians become entangled with the affairs of this life, the less they are entangled in the Spirit. The more Christians fight to maintain common ground with the world and be more accepting of the lifestyles of this world, the less the world will "know" us. Because the Church has not unified to combat the devil through the Spirit; the world is asking "who are you?" When the Body becomes unified within the Spirit realm, then churches will grow.

There is no more time for the big I's and little U's. It's time for us to see the mission that God has. It is true that each individual pastor has a unique vision, but we must understand that the vision comes from the Lord. When the Lord's collective vision is brought together, we will see a completely finished product. When we become unified in the Spirit, then we recognize what true vision is.

The
Benefit of
Christian
Maturity

CHAPTER 17

Joy, Peace, and Pleasures Evermore

I always marvel at those Christians who testify to how good God is and how long they've been saved, but are the meanest people you could ever meet. They have no joy. They are disheveled, easily agitated and nothing ever seems to go their way. This is not a sign of maturity.

Maturity is accompanied by a settling of behavior. As children, we were easily distracted by every little thing. We were jumpy and easily excited. As we matured, we became more focused. As Paul explained, "When I was a child, I spake as a child, I understood as a child, I thought as a child: but when I became a man, I put away childish things" (1 Cor. 13:11). The things we got excited about in the past no longer provoke arousal when we mature in Christ. We've learned more, so we adjust quicker to our changing environment.

"Joy"

When we become mature Christians, one of the signs others should see is that of joy. Psalm 16:11 states, "Thou wilt shew me the path of life: in thy presence is fullness of joy; at thy right hand there are pleasures for evermore." Some people feel as though they have to do something mystical to have the joy. Some people try to find the joy in material goods; cars, clothes, houses, but only "in thy presence" is fullness of joy.

One can only become a mature Christian by spending time in the presence of God. While in God's presence, by default, you begin to experience the joy. If someone claims to have just gotten out of a swimming pool, they should also be soaking wet. If they are not wet, then something is amiss. Likewise, when someone claims to be a mature Christian, but lacks joy, then something is amiss.

When should we have this joy? Should we have it when we are in the praise and worship session of the church service? Should we have it only when things are going well? No, we should have the joy of the Lord all of the time. In fact, we should have this joy even more so in the bad times because it is in the bad times that we should be in the presence of the Lord, more than any other time.

Of course you will not be happy every day, but joy and happiness are two different things. Happiness is momentary—contingent upon the situation, but joy is a lifestyle. For example: as a father, my children's behavior did not always make me happy. My sons, Jerry, Michael, and David, were true boys. In true boy fashion, they got into mischief. They broke things and made a mess. My daughter is strong willed and confident. This, at times, can be challenging to deal with for a father who doesn't want to see his little princess grow up. So you can imagine, I did not live in a perpetual state of happiness when it came to my children.

My children were always a joy to me. The joy of fatherhood was never missing. Whether or not my children obeyed, I found joy in looking at them; watching them grow and become independent. And even now, I may not be happy with every decision they make, but when I look at the great men and the great woman of God they have become; the joy I feel when I look at them is just as strong today, as the day I kissed their newborn heads.

Mature Christians should also have joy all the time. We should have the joy of life even when we are not happy with life's circumstances. We should have joy, knowing that we are resting in the center of God's perfect plan for our lives. We should have joy for the benefits of salvation. We should have joy because we are alive to experience the joys and pains of life. Even though life can be challenging, we are still very blessed to be able to endure the challenges of life.

More than the challenges of life, we can always look forward to the pleasures that God gives us. Mature Christians understand the pleasures that come after the pressures. They understand as Paul said they should "rejoice, inasmuch as ye are partakers of Christ's sufferings; that, when his glory shall be revealed, ye may be glad also with exceeding joy" (1 Pet. 4:13). Mature Christians find joy in the hardships of life, knowing the end result of their sufferings will be far greater than their pain.

"Peace"

Mature Christians have a peace "that passeth all understanding" (Phil 4:7). This peace is not a passive peace. In other words, I'm not talking about the peace that reflects a moment of ease; a time of relaxation or a time free of struggle. The peace I'm referring to is an active peace. It is a peace that is activated during a time where chaos reigns. Mature Christians have this active peace in the midst of struggle.

David experienced this peace. He said, "In my distress I called upon the LORD, and cried to my God: and he did hear my voice out of his temple, and my cry [did enter] into his ears" (2 Sam. 22:7). When his enemies were all around and look as though they will tear his life apart— David said, "By this I know that thou favourest me, because mine enemy doth not triumph over me." (Psa. 41:11).

Others look at the mature Christian and wonder why we sing. People can't fathom the peace of a mature Christian. If people are wondering why you have peace, that is an indication that you are going through what should be a very traumatic situation. Otherwise, people would not care how you responded.

Shadrach, Meshach, and Abednego are great examples of this peace. Nebuchadnezzar was so perplexed by these three young boys who seemed to have no fear of his threats. Here stood a king, who by most interpretations was a sociopath, who couldn't shake the resolve of three boys.

The three were so bold in the immanence of their demise that they told the king "we [are] not careful to answer thee in this matter" (Dan 3:16). In other words, they told this sociopath, "The conversation is over. We don't have to defend ourselves to you. If you're going to kill us, then let's get it over with already."

This so confused Nebuchadnezzar, it sent him into a rage. He ordered the heat of the fiery furnace to be heated so hot that it even killed his guards as they approached to throw the three in. Yet, even when they were thrown in the furnace, in the midst of the fire, they had peace. The Bible does not state Nebuchadnezzar looked in the furnace to find them cowering in a corner screaming. It states he saw "four men loose, walking in the midst of the fire" (v.25).

The three Hebrew boys had this peace because Jesus' presence was there and His presence transcended all human elements. When Christ is in you, He takes care of everything because everything is subject to Him. So in the midst of trouble, as you mature in Christ, you have peace.

"Pleasures Evermore"

When you learn how to submit yourself to God, you will find that there are pleasures evermore. As long as you live, there are pleasures. It's not miserable being in Christ. Jesus did say he had a yoke and a burden we must endure to follow Him. However, His "yoke is easy" and His "burden is light" (Matt. 11:30).

Some people have a hard time coming to the Church. It should not be hard coming to church—it ought to be pleasurable because you know when you join the Body there are pleasures evermore. There is a fullness of joy when you are in His presence; when the Shekinah glory is recognized in your midst; when the corporate anointing is present in your midst; then you know good things are going to happen. Why? Because His presence is there to help sustain you and to satisfy your needs. Every time there is a hurt, He is there to relieve you of your hurt; every time there is misery, He is there to lift you from your misery; every time you feel like you are going through, He is there to let you know, I'm here with you to take you through.

It may seem dark in your life, but God is your sunshine. It may seem like things are burdensome in your life, but God will lift your load for you. You may feel like you are friendless, but God is an everlasting friend. God is whatever you need. He is there for you. Whatever you want, just talk to Him and He'll give it to you, if it is what you need.

The Supreme Example of
Joy, Peace, and Pleasure Evermore

To culminate this chapter, let's look at the Prime example for walking in joy, peace and pleasure evermore. Jesus' every step was a lesson in Godly living. As we discuss these few attributes of mature Christians, we find they are only truly operative during times challenge or hardship.

Jesus' final hours of life provide us the greatest example for this chapter. At the age of 33, this young man literally had the weight of the entire world on His shoulders. Yes, He was God in the flesh, but He was also 100% human. The stress Jesus felt was so compelling, the Bible explains that Jesus "being in an agony he prayed more earnestly; and his sweat was as it were great drops of blood falling down to the ground" (Luke 22:44). Scientist have researched the plausibility of such a claim.

The scientific name for the condition is "**Hematidrosis.**" Hematidrosis is a rare condition in which a human being sweats blood. It occurs when a person is suffering extreme levels of stress; for example, facing his or her own death. It is very common for soldiers who are going into battle to sweat blood and for individuals who are unexpectedly given a death sentence.

My point is Jesus was not going on a hay ride. He was in a very stressful situation that would cause anyone unhappiness. The Bible does not say Jesus sweat blood, however, the circumstances He faced fit the description of a situation that would cause a person to sweat blood. Any person in Jesus' position would have full right to be scared out of his or her mind.

Jesus felt pain and knew how uncomfortable pain was. Jesus more than likely had witnessed a few crucifixions during His 33 years of life. He knew what was coming and it was not something He was looking forward to. At this point, Jesus was not happy with His fate. However, the joy He had in the Father was far greater than the happiness He would have experienced if that cup would have passed.

For one hour, Jesus prayed about the coming events. His crucifixion was at hand and he had the jitters—to put it lightly. He was stressed and asked "O my Father, if thou be willing, remove this cup from me; nevertheless not my will, but thine, be done" (Luke 22:42). In the midst of this stressful situation, there has to be a supernatural level of peace to conclude "nevertheless, not as I will." What peace did Jesus have? Jesus had peace in God's will. If our fates were subject to the roll of the dice; to the luck of chance; there would be very little about which to have peace. The reason we can have faith in the midst of the worst situations is because we have peace in the will of God. We know that God always has "plans to prosper you and not to harm you; plans to give you hope and a future" (Jeremiah 29:11). Because of this, our spirits rest at ease. Though the flesh may be petrified, our spirits are saying "Nevertheless, not as I will, but as you wilt." We notice that after praying, Jesus is cool, calm, and collected when the soldiers come to arrest Him.

What is True Pleasure?

Lastly, Jesus endured the worst punishment man has ever known because He knew what awaited Him—pleasures evermore. This pleasure He anticipated, however, was not a selfish pleasure. Yes, Jesus was being ushered to His thrown of eternal dominion where He would reign as King of kings, and Lord of lords, but this was not His only desire. Jesus' true pleasure was bringing salvation to His children. Herein lies the crux of Christian maturity—the understanding that your greatness is only found in what you do for your fellow man.

Jesus' pleasure was taking away the devil's authority. Jesus' pleasure came in the knowledge that the souls of men would be saved from eternal damnation. We, too, must find our pleasure in what we can do for others. If we are looking for pleasure to be personal gain, then we are sorely mistaken. No man will ever find true pleasure in amassing personal belongings. He or she will only find true fulfillment when he/she begins to give to others.

Jesus found pleasure evermore for the sacrifices He made to ensure the well being of others. We find in Him the prime example of walking in pleasure evermore through Christian maturity. We will find it only in God, and in what we do for others through God.

CHAPTER 18

Enjoying a Mature Christian Life

I believe that there is a Superior Being—A King of all worlds, all galaxies, and all of heaven and earth. I believe this King has all power and all majesty. And though I don't feel that we are equal to Him, I know that we are His heirs and in accordance with the Scripture, we are joint heirs with Jesus Christ. There is no reason for us to sit back and feel that we will never reach a level wherein we can enjoy being a part of the body of Christ.

It takes maturity to enjoy this Christian life. It takes maturity because this is not a fairytale where the world is your oyster and the riches of our Father allows us privileges to do whatever we like. On the contrary, to be a child of the King, you must endure a great deal of sacrifice. You don't get what you want; instead you get what you need for the Kingdom. Sometimes, what you need allows you to enjoy plenty, and sometimes what you need requires that you experience lack.

Living for God is not always fun, but you can still enjoy this Christian life.

If you are not enjoying your walk with the Lord, it is because you have not yet matured. You are frustrated often because of your lack of understanding of what being a part of the Church is. The Church does not at all diminish your posture in life. Rather, the Church enhances it. If you have not been enhanced in your living style, then you must question whether or not you understand who you are in the body of Christ and who the Lord is to you.

It's not a drag to be in the body of Christ; it's not complicated. We make it complicated because we try to live independently from Him. In other words, if we could understand that like the Richard Smallwood song explains: the Lord is the "source of our strength and the strength of our life" we would not struggle with living for God. If God is the source of your strength, then there's nothing you need to do to become strong. Furthermore, if He is the strength of your life, then He is actually doing all of the work. He provides the strength and then acts as the strength. All he needs from you is to be a willing vessel to stand in the gap.

For example, what did Moses really do? Moses didn't have the power to cause seven plagues. Moses didn't have the power to part the Red Sea. If we were to find Moses' rod today and stretched it over the Red Sea, that body of water would flow just as steady as it ever did. There was no power in the rod. All Moses did was act as a vessel. He simply said, "Hello

Pharaoh, God said 'Let my people go.'" That's it. However, Moses did have to endure the physical, mental, and emotional challenges of being that vessel. He did have to be the target for people's complaints. Beyond that, God did all of the work. Moses could take no credit.

Likewise, when we allow God to be the source of our strength and the strength of our lives, we can enjoy this life. We allow God this reign by allowing the Holy Spirit to rest, rule, and abide in us. The purpose of the Holy Ghost is to help you to become a witness; not through rhetorical exercise or articulation, but instead a witness as it relates to your behavior; a witness identified in the way you handle yourself each and every day. Acts 1:8 states,

> "But ye shall receive power after that the Holy Ghost is come upon you and ye shall be witnesses unto me both in Jerusalem and all Judea and in Samaria and to the uttermost part of the earth."

The Holy Ghost gives you power to witness or power to live; power to be exemplary in behavior or power to be Christ like so that others may desire to be like you.

He gives you power so that your life will not be miserable. The tasks you have in front of you are not difficult with God's power. This enabling force working within you, not outside of you, will help you to do what you are suppose to do and will release energy to help you when you cannot help yourself in the areas of love, peace, joy, patience. God wants you to know that you can mature to an extent that you are able to stand firmly on His Word and allow the world to see that being in Him is exciting, productive, and empowering.

In Christ, you have *DUNAMIS* power— the ability of God. I'm not talking about something that's placed upon you like an electrical current, The power of God remains. There is not an on and off switch. This power lasts longer than the Energizer Bunny®. 2 Kings 13:21 shows us how long-lasting this power is. After the prophet Elisha died, this scripture tells us at the "coming in of the year" a band of Moabites invaded the land. The Moabites were burying a man, unbeknownst to them, in the sepulcher of Elisha. When the dead man touched Elisha's bones—not the corpse, but the decomposed skeletal bones of the prophet— the dead man leaped from the grave.

This is the same power that Christ had and the power He gives us. Many people still may find this Christian power hard to believe because they don't readily see the tangible benefits of the Christian life—material goods. We are consumed with consumption in American society which has become a major hindrance to the Body. If the Apostle Paul were speaking, he would say that we have "become entangled with the affairs of this life" (2 Tim. 2:4). He would continue and say we have fulfilled his prophecy and we "will not endure sound doctrine; but after our own lusts have heaped to ourselves teachers, having itching ears" (2 Tim. 4:3). We have gorged ourselves on prosperity, blessings, and all the "goodies" of Christian living. We have stunted our maturity and disillusioned those who join the Body.

Converts are not enjoying Christianity because we are not teaching scriptures like Romans 5:3 "we glory in tribulation; knowing that tribulation worketh patience"; or Philippians 4:11 "For I have learned, in whatsoever state I am, therewith to be content." Instead we focus on verse 13 "I can do all things through Christ which strengtheneth me." Converts go out and try to "do all things" only to come back rejected and discouraged because not *all* things will strengthen.

They misread this scripture and interpreted it to mean "I can do all things through Christ WHO strengthens me." The pronoun "who" shifts the responsibility of "doing all things" on Christ. We therefore interpret this to mean we can do ANYTHING as long as we are in Christ. However, we should focus on the word "which." The word "which" is used to represent inanimate items, circumstances, events, etc. So when we say I can do all things through Christ "which" strengthens me, we are not talking about Christ, but instead the event, circumstance or phenomenon.

I can do all things through Christ "which" strengthens me, really means I can endure any event WHICH WILL strengthen me. I can endure any circumstance which will strengthen me. If I can rephrase it, we should understand this scripture to read "I can do all things *that will* strengthen me through Christ", as opposed to the more common interpretation, "I can do all things through Christ who is going to strengthen me to do it." With this translation, I no longer feel I can do anything I set my heart to do just because I'm in Christ. Instead I ask Christ, "is this event going to strengthen me and my purpose in the Kingdom?" If so, then I know that I can do it through Christ.

For example; If I decide I want to become the richest man in America, I must ask God if that is really going to strengthen me. Although it may strengthen my purchasing power and my influence in society, will it strengthen my spirit man? Will I become less focused on God and more focused on maintaining, protecting, and increasing my massive wealth? Will it strengthen my relationships with my family, friends and others? Many times, the more money one acquires the more stress comes into his/her relationships. So this scripture is not referring to a carnal, materialistic or physical strengthening, but instead a spiritual strengthening. We can do all things through Christ which strengthens us to be more mature Christians.

In the context of this letter to the Philippians, we find Paul discussing how much he appreciated the Philippians willingness to help him in his present afflictions. This was not what we would call a time of prosperity and peace for Paul. Paul explains that he has learned to be content in whatever plight he finds himself. He explains that he has learned that he can endure the event or circumstance of abounding or abasement through Christ. These events will strengthen him, so through Christ, He can endure.

Paul was able to enjoy his Christian walk even in times of what seemed like complete destitution because he was able to understand that he had all he needed in the Spirit. He had access by faith to the grace of God and everything that he needed was in God's grace. Today, everything you need is within God's grace. You have the power today. You don't have to exercise everyday for God's power. You don't have to practice incantations. You have power to live and enjoy your life by simply allowing God's power to live in you through the Holy Ghost. Simply do what He tells you to do. Be the empty vessel Christ needs and you will enjoy a powerful, mature Christian life.

More About Bishop Jerry L. Maynard

Bishop Maynard completed graduate and postgraduate studies in Psychology and Social Sciences at Indiana University and the Doctorates Division of Cross Roads Bible College. Bishop Maynard, a native of Indiana, served as Director of the Muncie Indiana Human Rights Commission from 1967-1970, a member of the Indiana and United States Civil Rights Commission from 1970-1981, and the President's Domestic Policy Committee from 1977-1983. He is the recipient of the highest civilian award of the state of Indiana, "Sagamore of the Wabash."

A noted speaker, Bishop Maynard has lectured at Ball State University, Taylor University, Indiana and Indiana State Universities, Cross Roads Bible College, Clark University and keynoted the nationally know "Soul Winners" Conference.

Bishop Maynard's concern for the growth and edification of God's people extends beyond the church. In 1997, as Cathedral Of Praise (formerly Pentecostal Tabernacle) began planning for the construction of the new 1800 seat Sanctuary and Worship Center, Bishop Maynard chose Church Builders United, a partnership of minority-owned contractors. In addition, minority and women-owned businesses worked as sub-contractors on the project.

Bishop Maynard further insisted that the labor force be made up of a significant number of minorities. Thus, approximately eighty-percent of the laborers working on the construction of the facility were African-American and Latino. Other churches building new facilities are now patterning this model. For his efforts, and his many contributions for the establishment of entrepreneurial enterprises, Bishop Maynard received the "R. H. Boyd Business Advocate of the Year 1999" award.

Bishop Maynard, a pioneer in ministry, utilizes new technology and the media to reach the masses. The Cathedral of Praise daily radio broadcasts, weekly telecast on Cable/TV, and website are ways in which Bishop Maynard delivers his messages of "Maximizing Your Potential."

Bishop Maynard is married to Dr. Mary T. Maynard who is retired from serving as Deputy Superintendent of Schools in DeKalb County Georgia.

NOTES

NOTES

NOTES